"The biblical teaching on the priesthood seems foreign and forbidding to many readers today. David Schrock helps us see how a theology of the priesthood permeates the storyline of the Bible and how the priesthood climaxes in Christ and finds its fulfillment in him."

Thomas R. Schreiner, James Buchanan Harrison Professor of New Testament Interpretation, The Southern Baptist Theological Seminary

"David Schrock helps Christ's royal priesthood exult in Christ, the supreme royal priest."

Andrew Naselli, Associate Professor of Systematic Theology and New Testament, Bethlehem College and Seminary

"With the recent surge in biblical-theological studies, especially thematic developments across the canon, it is a little surprising that the theme of priesthood has not received more attention. David Schrock's work fills this gap beautifully! Specifically, this book probes the significance of the priesthood for a precise understanding of the gospel, as well as our own calling as royal priests through Jesus. Essential reading on this major biblical theme!"

Nicholas G. Piotrowski, President and Academic Dean, Indianapolis Theological Seminary

"Schrock has given us an absolutely fresh analysis and perspective on priesthood through the lens of biblical theology. While some may find his proposals provocative at times, none who read these pages—layperson or scholar—will fail to benefit from his study."

Peter J. Gentry, Distinguished Visiting Professor of Old Testament, Phoenix Seminary

"Identity formation is a pressing challenge facing the church in this generation. David Schrock has provided vital aid for this task by drawing attention to the church's true identity as a royal priesthood. I have waited for a book like this for two decades. May all who read it have their eyes opened to the transforming power of participation in Christ's royal priesthood."

Hank Voss, Assistant Professor of Christian Ministries, Taylor University

T0339256

The Royal Priesthood and the Glory of God

Short Studies in Biblical Theology

Edited by Dane C. Ortlund and Miles V. Van Pelt

The Royal Priesthood and the Glory of God

David S. Schrock

WHEATON, ILLINOIS

The Royal Priesthood and the Glory of God

Copyright © 2022 by David S. Schrock

Published by Crossway
        1300 Crescent Street
        Wheaton, Illinois 60187

Cover design: Jordan Singer

First printing 2022

Printed in the United States of America

Unless otherwise indicated, Scripture quotations are from the ESV® Bible (The Holy Bible, English Standard Version®), copyright © 2001 by Crossway, a publishing ministry of Good News Publishers. Used by permission. All rights reserved.

Scripture marked KJV is from the King James Version of the Bible. Public domain.

Scripture marked NASB is from *The New American Standard Bible*®. Copyright © 1960, 1962, 1963, 1968, 1971, 1972, 1973, 1975, 1977, 1995 by The Lockman Foundation. Used by permission. www.Lockman.org.

Scripture quotations designated NET are from the NET Bible® copyright © 1996–2016 by Biblical Studies Press, L.L.C. http://netbible.com. Used by permission. All rights reserved.

Scripture marked NKJV is taken from the New King James Version®. Copyright © 1982 by Thomas Nelson. Used by permission. All rights reserved.

All emphases in Scripture quotations have been added by the author.

Trade paperback ISBN: 978-1-4335-6431-4
ePub ISBN: 978-1-4335-6434-5
PDF ISBN: 978-1-4335-6432-1
Mobipocket ISBN: 978-1-4335-6433-8

Library of Congress Cataloging-in-Publication Data

Names: Schrock, David S., 1980– author. | Ortlund, Dane Calvin, editor. | Van Pelt, Miles V., 1969– editor.
Title: The royal priesthood and the glory of God / David S. Schrock.
Description: Wheaton, Illinois : Crossway, 2022. | Series: Short studies in biblical theology | Includes bibliographical references and index.
Identifiers: LCCN 2021009707 (print) | LCCN 2021009708 (ebook) | ISBN 9781433564314 (trade paperback) | ISBN 9781433564321 (pdf) | ISBN 9781433564338 (mobi) | ISBN 9781433564345 (epub)
Subjects: LCSH: Priesthood—Biblical teaching.
Classification: LCC BS680.P66 S37 2022 (print) | LCC BS680.P66 (ebook) | DDC 232/.8—dc23
LC record available at https://lccn.loc.gov/2021009707
LC ebook record available at https://lccn.loc.gov/2021009708

Crossway is a publishing ministry of Good News Publishers.

BP		31	30	29	28	27	26	25	24	23	22
15	14	13	12	11	10	9	8	7	6	5	4	3	2	1

To the family of royal priests
who gather at Occoquan Bible Church

Contents

Illustrations

Figures

Tables

Series Preface

Most of us tend to approach the Bible early on in our Christian lives as a vast, cavernous, and largely impenetrable book. We read the text piecemeal, finding golden nuggets of inspiration here and there, but remain unable to plug any given text meaningfully into the overarching storyline. Yet one of the great advances in evangelical biblical scholarship over the past few generations has been the recovery of biblical theology—that is, a renewed appreciation for the Bible as a theologically unified, historically rooted, progressively unfolding, and ultimately Christ-centered narrative of God's covenantal work in our world to redeem sinful humanity.

This renaissance of biblical theology is a blessing, yet little of it has been made available to the general Christian population. The purpose of Short Studies in Biblical Theology is to connect the resurgence of biblical theology at the academic level with everyday believers. Each volume is written by a capable scholar or churchman who is consciously writing in a way that requires no prerequisite theological training of the reader. Instead, any thoughtful Christian disciple can track with and benefit from these books.

Each volume in this series takes a whole-Bible theme and traces it through Scripture. In this way readers not only learn about a given theme but also are given a model for how to read the Bible as a coherent whole.

We have launched this series because we love the Bible, we love the church, and we long for the renewal of biblical theology in the academy to enliven the hearts and minds of Christ's disciples all around the world. As editors, we have found few discoveries more thrilling in life than that of seeing the whole Bible as a unified story of God's gracious acts of redemption, and indeed of seeing the whole Bible as ultimately about Jesus, as he himself testified (Luke 24:27; John 5:39).

The ultimate goal of Short Studies in Biblical Theology is to magnify the Savior and to build up his church—magnifying the Savior through showing how the whole Bible points to him and his gracious rescue of helpless sinners; and building up the church by strengthening believers in their grasp of these life-giving truths.

Dane C. Ortlund and Miles V. Van Pelt

Introduction

Recovering the Glory of the Royal Priesthood

In 1956 the film *The Ten Commandments* showed a generation of Americans a picture of the Passover, the Red Sea, and God's relationship with Israel. With cinematic flare Charlton Heston, portraying Moses, battled Pharaoh, led the people to Sinai, and smashed the stone tablets in response to the golden calf. On the silver screen, *The Ten Commandments* portrayed a vision of God's glory as told through the story of the exodus. Yet, every Easter when it plays on television, *The Ten Commandments* can never fully capture the glory of God. Why? Because it takes more than good camera work to see God's glory. It requires the Spirit to open sin-blinded eyes to behold the glory of God in the face of Jesus Christ (2 Cor. 4:6).

From the New Testament, we can see more clearly why *The Ten Commandments* misses the mark. The ancient glory of exodus cannot display God's glory without the final revelation of God in Christ. As the New Testament explains, God designed the exodus to foreshadow the later glory of Christ. As Paul puts it, Moses's face shone with glory when he descended from Sinai (2 Cor. 3:7), but this glory paled in comparison to Christ's. With Moses, God's glory was found in a ministry of condemnation, but with Christ, glory is seen in his ministry of righteousness (2 Cor. 3:9–11). Righteousness is what Christ grants his people by means of his covenantal obedience, sacrificial death, victorious resurrection, and heavenly intercession. In other words, through the various phases of Christ's priesthood, the glory of God is fully revealed. And not just revealed but given. Whereas Moses's priestly ministry displayed God's glory from a distance, the greater ministry of Christ clothes his people with righteousness, as the greater high priest brings many sons to glory (Heb. 2:9–10; cf. Rom. 8:29–31).

Consider how vital this priestly vision of God's glory is for ministry today. From the athletic arena to the concert stage to the IMAX theater, countless worshipers flock to experience the glory of sport, song, and cinema. As Jamie Smith has observed, venues like these provide a series of secular temples complete with their own idolatrous liturgies.[1] Set in these temples are a priestly class of people who distribute "grace" to a world hungry for glory. And just as Charlton Heston once entertained a generation of glory-seekers, so today's athletes and entertainers regale modern inquirers. These cultural icons are the priests of our secular age, and they bestow glory on all who draw near to them, wear their signature brands, and enter their temples. Nevertheless, their "priestly" services only mislead their followers from true glory, even as they confirm a basic truth—fallen humanity requires priestly intervention to restore the glory we were made to receive and reflect.

Priestly glory is also found when we enter the Bible. From the first use of the word in Genesis 14:18 ("Melchizedek . . . was *priest* of God Most High") to the last in Revelation 20:6 ("Blessed and holy is the one who shares in the first resurrection! . . . they will

---

1. James K. A. Smith, *Desiring the Kingdom: Worship, Worldview, and Cultural Formation* (Grand Rapids, MI: Baker Academic, 2009).

be *priests* of God and of Christ"), priesthood is central to redemptive history. And though it takes some time to learn the language, the concepts, and the purpose of priesthood, a pleasant reward awaits all who study what Scripture says about priesthood. As Psalm 111:2 says,

> Great are the works of the LORD,
>   studied by all who delight in them.

The aim of this book is to study the priesthood so that we might delight more fully in the glory of God's Son, our great high priest. Moreover, by learning the history and purpose of priesthood in the Bible, we will better understand God's work in redemption. Because God's gospel of the kingdom centers on the priestly offering and exaltation of Christ, a right understanding of royal priesthood is necessary for seeing God's glorious plan of salvation. Because the church of Jesus Christ is called to share in his vocation of priesthood (1 Pet. 2:5, 9; Rev. 5:9–10), learning what priests do is essential for discipleship.

In a world of competing glories, therefore, studying the priesthood is basic for Christian discipleship. When secular priests entice Christians to worship in their temples, we need the true priest-king interceding for us and applying his blood to atone for our sins. We need a biblical vision of Christ's priestly glory to empower us to reject all substitutes and worship him alone. In short, we need a biblical theology of royal priesthood that leads us to Christ. For to be made in God's image and created for God's glory means Christ's disciples are called to be a family of royal priests—sons and daughters who serve in the presence of the Lord by means of the finished work of Christ, our great high priest.

That's the big picture; now let me define a few priestly terms.

A Glorious Family of Royal Priests

If we survey all the places where priests show up in the Bible, we find quite a spectrum. There are pagan priests like Potiphera, the father-in-law of Joseph (Gen. 41:45, 50; 46:20), and true priests like Melchizedek (Gen. 14:18). Aaron and his sons are identified as Israel's chosen line of priests, and these priests are joined by their brothers, the Levites, to serve in God's tabernacle (cf. Deut. 33:8–11). Yet, before Yahweh chose Aaron as priest (Ex. 28–29), Yahweh identified Israel as a "royal priesthood" (Ex. 19:6). Likewise, when Moses led the nation to make a covenant with Yahweh (Ex. 19–24), unnamed "priests" served at the altar with Moses (19:22, 24; cf. 24:5). Moses too is identified as a priest, as is Samuel (Ps. 99:6). Yet neither is a descendant of Aaron or called a priest in his own day. Moreover, David wears the priestly ephod when the ark of the covenant is brought to Jerusalem (2 Sam. 6:14), and in one instance his sons are even called "priests" (2 Sam. 8:18).

Despite the "separation of powers" between the priestly tribe of Levi and the royal tribe of Judah, we discover royal sons who bring sacrifices to the altar. This combination of priest and king goes back to Adam and Melchizedek. And looking in the other direction, the prophets tell of a son of David who will be priest (Ps. 110) and a priest who will sit on the throne (Zech. 6:9–15). Admittedly, all these twists and turns can seem daunting at first. But if we read the Bible patiently, we can learn how the priesthood rises and falls and rises again.

Already, this series has books devoted to the themes of sonship and kingdom.[2] So this book will not repeat their work. Still, it is necessary to see how priesthood relates to both. To say it differently,

---

2. Graeme Goldsworthy, *The Son of God and the New Creation*, Short Studies in Biblical Theology (Wheaton, IL: Crossway, 2015); Patrick Schreiner, *The Kingdom of God and the Glory of the Cross*, Short Studies in Biblical Theology (Wheaton, IL: Crossway, 2018).

priesthood is restricted to the sons of Aaron only under the law of Moses, explicated in the covenant with Levi (Num. 25:9–13; Mal. 2:1–9; cf. Deut. 33:8–11). Prior to the Sinai, Scripture identifies *royal* priests in Adam and his sons, the patriarchs. Israel, as God's firstborn son (Ex. 4:22–23) is also called a "kingdom of priests" (Ex. 19:6). And many of the patriarchs, who were promised a kingdom (Gen. 17:6, 16), built altars—a task later associated with Aaron and his sons. In the beginning then, there is a strong unity between priest and king.

This unity will fracture in Israel's history, but when Jesus fulfills the requirements of the law, he will become a priest like the king of Salem, Melchizedek. David himself saw this coming (Pss. 110; 132), as did the Old Testament prophets (e.g., Jer. 30:21; Zech. 3:1–10; 6:9–15). Thus, the church is not simply a priestly people. In Christ, it is a *royal* priesthood. To put it graphically, we might say Aaron's priesthood, which would come to be known as the Levitical priesthood, always stood as a halfway house between Adam's royal priesthood and Christ's (see fig. 1).

Figure 1. Israel's temporary division of priesthood from kingship

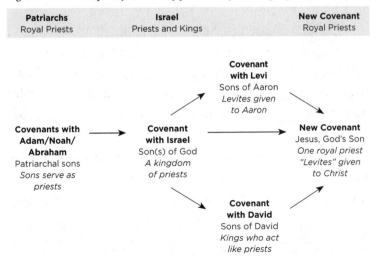

As with the rest of the law, the priesthood of Aaron was not an end in itself; it was given as a pattern and placeholder for something greater—namely, Jesus Christ and the royal priesthood he would inaugurate through his death and resurrection. To be certain, it takes the whole Bible to see this develop, but as we begin, we need to see where we are going. In particular, it is vital to see the historical development of priesthood in relationship to kingship. To help explain how these concepts relate, let me define them.

Priest. Hebrews provides the most detailed explanation of priesthood in the Bible. And in Hebrews 5:1–4 we find a concise definition of the high priest, his appointment, his people, and his service:

> For every high priest chosen from among men is appointed to act on behalf of men in relation to God, to offer gifts and sacrifices for sins. He can deal gently with the ignorant and wayward, since he himself is beset with weakness. Because of this he is obligated to offer sacrifice for his own sins just as he does for those of the people. And no one takes this honor for himself, but only when called by God, just as Aaron was.

From these verses, we can draft a working definition of priesthood in four parts. First, Hebrews defines a "high priest" (5:1), which is the term given to the sons of Aaron in Numbers 35. This identification does not encompass everything we can say about priests, but it does provide a start. Second, a high priest is chosen by God and does not appoint himself (Heb. 5:1, 4). This received ministry repeatedly identifies true priests. No priest in the Bible ever asserts himself before God and lives to tell about it. God always does the choosing and the consecrating for service at his altar. Third, God appoints the high priest to serve a particular people and to mediate a covenant.[3] So great

---

3. Notice again the close relationship between priesthood and covenant in figure 1.

was the priest's place in the covenant, Hebrews 7:12 says, "When there is a change in the priesthood, there is necessarily a change in the law as well." Notice: the change in the law followed the change in priesthood, not the reverse. Fourth and finally, priests brought sacrifices for sin to the altar of God. While all Israelites worshiped God with sacrifices, the priest applied the blood to the altar. Under the Sinai covenant, this task was reserved for Aaron and his sons. Not even Levites could serve at the altar. Yet, before Sinai, the sons of Adam and Abraham built altars, made sacrifices, and applied the blood. These actions identify them as patriarchal priests.

In defining what a priest is, Hebrews 5 gives a clear starting point: *Priests are consecrated mediators between God and his covenant people who stand to serve at God's altar and bring sacrifices to atone for sin.* Yet, as Hebrews 5 focuses on Israel's high priest, we should remember that more can be said. From what we will see in the Old Testament itself, I will define priesthood in this way: *Priests are consecrated mediators between God and his covenant people, who stand to serve at God's altar (1) sanctifying God's Holy Place, (2) sacrificing God's offerings, and (3) speaking God's covenant.*[4]

This more expansive definition considers *where* priests serve and *what* priests do. Namely, priests *sanctify* the house of God where the altar is located; they *bring the sacrificial blood* to that altar; and they *bless the people with their speech*—for example, intercessory prayer, benediction, and teaching are priestly activities. More could be said, but this definition gets at the heart of what priests do. Others have defined priests by where they stand—as servants in God's house.[5] As we go, we will see the importance of where the priests stand, but our

---

4. This definition is unique to the sons of Aaron. Levites, by contrast, do not stand at God's altar, but serve as assistants to Aaron, guarding God's house (not his altar) and carrying the word of the covenant to the people. In this way, they too are "priestly," but not "priests" in the official sense of the word.

5. Peter J. Leithart, "Attendants of Yahweh's House: Priesthood in the Old Testament," *Journal for the Study of the Old Testament* 24, no. 85 (1999): 3–24.

focus will be on what priests do—that is, priestly actions. And this definition will be a guide throughout the book.

Levitical priesthood. In the law, priesthood came to be associated with Aaron and the house of Levi. In Hebrews we find the term "Levitical priesthood," which—counterintuitively—does not mean all the Levites but refers only to the sons of Aaron. As Hebrews 7:11 explains, "Levitical priesthood" is another way of describing the "order of Aaron." As we will see, priesthood is given only to Aaron and his sons. Later the sons of Levi will be "given" to Aaron, to protect him and to assist him at God's house (Num. 3:9; 8:16, 19; 18:8), but the term itself ("Levitical priesthood") does not appear until Deuteronomy.[6] "Levitical priesthood," therefore, is a term that speaks of the entire priestly system centered on Aaron and his offspring.

Under the old covenant, the priestly "order of Aaron" is the one that serves at the altar. The Levites stand with them to protect God's house, assist God's priests, and serve God's people. Importantly, this system of mediation is the one established by Moses; it is also the one that Jesus confronts as he speaks of the temple's defilement and coming destruction. In between Moses and Jesus, the Levitical priesthood serves as Israel's thermostat for worship. For as it goes with the priests so goes the spiritual climate of the nation.

Royal priesthood. Hebrews also speaks of a priesthood that supersedes that of Aaron. This priesthood is described as the "order of Melchizedek" (Heb. 7:11), the king of Salem and priest of God Most High (cf. Heb. 7:1–10). Though he is identified only in Genesis 14 and Psalm 110, Hebrews makes Melchizedek the key figure to explain how Jesus can be a priest. In this book, we will see how Melchizedek is the major figure in a biblical theology of priesthood.

---

6. See Deut. 17:9, 18; 18:1; 24:8; 27:9; cf. 21:5; 31:9.

To rightly trace the priesthood through the Bible, it is important to see that the goal of priesthood is a *royal* priest. Priesthood decoupled from kingship is not the final goal. As Hebrews teaches, God always intended to replace the covenant with Israel (and its covenant with Levi) with a new covenant—the covenant inaugurated by a king invited by God to "draw near" (Jer. 30:21).[7]

Priesthood tied to the tribe of Levi, therefore, was always provisional. As we will see, God created Adam to serve as a priest *and* to have rule over the earth. The priests and kings of Israel, taken by themselves, recover only "half" of what Adam lost by his disobedience. Like Adam, God gave Israel the chance to be a "royal priesthood" *if they kept the covenant* (Ex. 19:1–8). Yet, because the nation broke God's covenant, Israel proved themselves unfit to be a royal priesthood. Nevertheless, what God promised conditionally to Israel, Christ fulfilled perfectly. And only as we keep track of the Bible's presentation of priesthood *and* kingship can we rightly make sense of Scripture's view of priesthood.

The Glory of the Priesthood

In this book, we will focus on the glory seen in the beauty of God's house and its priestly servants. Once again, Hebrews is instructive. In Hebrews 3:1–6 we find a contrast between the glory of Moses and the glory of Jesus. Both are glorious in their respective roles—Moses serving in God's house, Jesus ruling over God's house. This glory comes from the work each does with the resulting effects of their priestly service.

Truly, Christ's glory begins with the purifying power of his priestly sacrifice. It continues with the high priest enthroned in heaven, who

---

7. "Drawing near," which repeats often in Hebrews (4:16; 7:19, 25; 10:1, 22; 11:6), is a priestly phrase, one that comes from the priest's God-given permission to approach God's altar (cf. Ex. 28:1).

lives to intercede for his household. And it extends to all the earth as he sends the gospel throughout creation. In these three ways (sacrifice, sanctification, and speaking), we see the beauty and glory of Christ's perfect priesthood. In the chapters that follow, we will trace Christ's priestly glory through the Bible, learning how a biblical theology of priesthood informs our own discipleship as royal priests.

Still, before jumping in, let me outline the six chapters of this book. Each chapter corresponds to one of six stages in the development of the priesthood:

1. The *pattern of royal priesthood* in Adam and the patriarchs
2. The *legislation of the Levitical priesthood* in the five books of Moses (Genesis–Deuteronomy)
3. The *compromise of the Levitical priesthood* and the *promise of a royal priesthood* in the Prophets (Joshua, Judges, 1–2 Samuel, 1–2 Kings, Isaiah, Jeremiah, Ezekiel, and the Twelve[8])
4. The *rising anticipation of a royal priesthood* in the Writings (1–2 Chronicles, Ezra–Nehemiah, Psalms, and Daniel)
5. The *arrival of the royal priest(hood)* in the Gospels (Matthew–John)
6. The *meaning and multiplication of the royal priesthood* in Acts through Revelation

While the biblical story of priesthood has many moving parts, these six escalating stages help us stay on track. Like a map that identifies various regions with a corresponding color, these six stages will help color each chapter of our journey. In this way, the details of this story, which become dense at times, can be organized by these stages.

---

8. The Twelve are the "Minor Prophets" taken collectively.

In all, this book will chronicle the hard-but-ultimately-happy history of God's royal priesthood. At the end of our journey, we will find a vision of royal priests worshiping God and serving alongside Jesus Christ. This is the goal of the Bible and the goal of creation, but long before seeing the glory of God's new Jerusalem, we must start in Eden—the place where royal priesthood begins.

1

In the Beginning

The Royal Priesthood Patterned

In the beginning God created a priest. And not just any priest, but a royal priest—a man made in God's likeness, a son fashioned to reflect God's beauty, an image bearer commissioned to rule God's world with holy affections. God commissioned the first family—Adam and his fellow image bearer, Eve—to be fruitful and multiply and fill the world with God's glory.

The first few chapters of Genesis bring the reader into a foreign world with many ancient places, practices, and people. Presented as symbol-laden history, Genesis tells us where humanity came from, why we are here, and what went wrong. It also hints at who will "fix" it. This is where the Bible begins, and so does our priestly journey. In this chapter we will observe the pattern of royal priesthood found in Adam and his sons. In particular, we will see how priesthood begins with Adam, echoes in the patriarchs (esp.

Abraham), and finds its most concrete yet enigmatic example in Melchizedek.

While priesthood is not defined or assigned until Sinai, we can see how priesthood in Israel finds an original pattern in Genesis. Indeed, by reading Genesis with the rest of the Pentateuch (Exodus–Deuteronomy), we learn how Moses portrays these men as patriarchal priests, which in turn gives us an original pattern for royal priesthood.

Evidence for the First Priest

Genesis 1–2 presents Eden as a garden sanctuary and the first man as royal priest. Later, after humanity's fall (Gen. 3), sacrifice will be added to complete the cultic system. Together, the indivisible complex of sanctuary, priesthood, and sacrifice begins in Genesis 1–3.[1]

As we observed in the introduction, even secular societies participate in cultic worship. Malls, models, and merchandise form a materialistic cult alluring worshipers to make a sacrifice at the altar of Apple or REI. Similarly, worship in the Bible requires a Holy Place (a temple), a devoted priesthood, and a sacrifice on the altar.[2] As strange as ancient religions may look, patterns of priestly worship still surround us. And going back to Eden, we discover why. In fact, Moses gives at least four ways to see priesthood in Eden.

First, Adam is placed in a garden sanctuary. Set on a mountain where the waters flowed down from Eden, the "garden of God" (Isa.

---

1. G. K. Beale, *The Temple and the Church's Mission: A Biblical Theology of the Dwelling Place of God*, New Studies in Biblical Theology (Downers Grove, IL: InterVarsity Press, 2004), 81–121; T. Desmond Alexander, *The City of God and the Goal of Creation*, Short Studies in Biblical Theology (Wheaton, IL: Crossway, 2018), 18–20.

2. This does not deny Jesus's words in John 4:21, "The hour is coming when neither on this mountain nor in Jerusalem will you worship the Father." Rather, under the new covenant God's worshipers do not worship in one place; they gather in every place (1 Cor. 1:2; cf. Mal. 1:11). But in every place, those worshipers come to Mount Zion (Heb. 12:22) when they assemble as God's living temple, locally gathered by God's Spirit.

51:3; Ezek. 28:13; 31:9) was the place where Adam and Eve enjoyed Yahweh's presence. While Eden was a perfect environment for man to dwell, Genesis 1–2 is theological, not agricultural. The garden was far more than verdant farmland; it was the place where God approached Adam, and Adam entered God's presence—hence a garden sanctuary.

Like the tabernacle, which had three spheres of increasing holiness (the courtyard, the Holy Place, and the Most Holy Place), Eden also had three regions of ascending holiness (the world outside the garden, the garden itself, and the top of God's mountain, where his presence dwelt). In all, God created Adam and all of his children in his image to commune with him and to serve as his priests in his Holy Place.[3]

Second, image bearers are royal priests who mediate God's presence. Genesis 1:26–28 says God made humanity in his own image and likeness. And while Adam and Eve's royal function is observable in the words "subdue" and "have dominion over" in verse 28, there is reason to assign priesthood to these words too. In the ancient Near East, image bearing was inherently priestly, as the king mediated the presence of God to the people and vice versa. Similarly, Adam plays a priestly role whereby he mediates the relationship between God and his children.[4] The blessing Adam receives from God (v. 28) is to be communicated to his family as he serves as their priest. Conversely, standing as the head of his family, he is to lead them to worship and serve their Creator. All of this fails when Adam sins, but in Genesis 1–2 we can see God's original intent. Even more, when we read 1:26–28 with 2:15, it becomes clearer that Adam, as God's image bearer, is commissioned to be a priest.

---

3. Beale, *The Temple and the Church's Mission*, 75; Beale, "Adam as the First Priest in Eden as the Garden Temple," *Southern Baptist Journal of Theology* 22, no. 2 (2018): 9–24.

4. These children would also bear the image of God, communicated to them through their father (see Gen. 5:1–2).

Third, Adam is given a priestly commission. Genesis 2 says that when God planted a garden in Eden (v. 8), "The LORD God took the man and put him in the garden of Eden to *work* it and *keep* it" (v. 15). Adding to the ruling commands of Genesis 1:28, Adam is given the priestly task of "serving" Yahweh in his garden sanctuary and "guarding" his sacred space. We know this double command (i.e., "work/serve" combined with "keep/guard") is priestly because of the way Moses uses it later in Numbers 3:7–8; 8:25–26; 18:5–7. In Numbers these two words, when used together, are uniquely assigned to the Levites, who are called to assist in the priestly service of the tabernacle.[5]

Adam is therefore presented in priestly terms. He is "an archetypal Levite."[6] Confirming his priesthood, God calls him to serve in his presence and to guard the boundaries of his holy space from anything unclean.[7] Later, Levites are called "guards" (1 Chron. 9:23) and "gatekeepers" (1 Chron. 9:17–27; Neh. 11:19). Moreover, the Levites' service begins because of their willingness to draw the sword against their brothers to defend God's holiness (Ex. 32:25–29; Deut. 33:8–11). Such zeal for God's holy dwelling is a defining characteristic of priests and Levites, and in the beginning, God assigns Adam to be guardian of the garden sanctuary.

Fourth, the rest of the Bible presents Adam as a priest. When Moses identifies Aaron and his sons as the chosen priests of Israel (Ex. 28–29), he makes multiple connections between the creation of the world (Gen. 1–2) and the fabrication of the tabernacle (Ex. 25–31). For instance, both passages are organized by seven

---

5. Beale, "Adam as the First Priest," 10.

6. Kenneth Mathews, *Genesis 1–11:26*, New American Commentary (Nashville: B&H, 1996), 52; see also Peter J. Gentry and Stephen J. Wellum, *Kingdom through Covenant: A Biblical-Theological Understanding of the Covenants* (Wheaton, IL: Crossway, 2012), 211–13.

7. Beale, *The Temple and the Church's Mission*, 69.

divine words—that is, seven divine acts of creation formed the cosmos, and seven divine words organized the tabernacle.[8] Thus, "the tabernacle is portrayed as a reconstruction of God's good creation."[9] Similarly, the six days of creation, which led to the seventh day of "rest" (Gen. 2:1–3), prefigure the construction of the tabernacle and appointment of Aaron to stand at the altar, which is associated with Sabbath (Ex. 31:12–18).

Additionally, God designed the tabernacle to reflect the floral beauty of Eden, and the priestly garments to point back to Adam. As Moses wrote for a people whose worship centered on priests clothed in beauty and glory (Ex. 28:2), these glorious garments capture a vision of the Edenic priest (see Ezek. 28:11–14). As we will see in chapter 2, Aaron's priestly attire includes a golden crown (Ex. 29:6; 39:30), a golden ephod (Ex. 28:6–14), and onyx shoulder pieces with the names of the twelve tribes engraved on them (Ex. 28:9–11). Strikingly, gold and onyx are found in Eden (Gen. 2:12), making another connection between Aaron and Adam.[10]

In these ways, Moses demonstrates how the formation of the world is temple-like (cf. Ps. 104), and the fabrication of the tabernacle is creation-like. Accordingly, when Aaron is given access to the tabernacle, it is as if a new Adam has reentered God's garden. Whereas the first priest compromised God's command and failed in his priestly commission, God begins anew with Aaron to recover what Adam lost. Indeed, when we see the connections between Aaron and Adam, we begin to see how the original pattern of priesthood is meant to inform the rest of the Bible.

---

8. See Gen. 1:3, 6, 9, 14, 20, 24, 26; cf. 1:11, 28, 29 and Ex. 25:1; 30:11, 17, 22, 34; 31:1, 12.

9. See John H. Sailhamer, *The Pentateuch as Narrative: A Biblical-Theological Commentary* (Grand Rapids, MI: Zondervan, 1995), 298–99.

10. For more on the relationship between Aaron and Adam, see Michael Morales, *Who Shall Ascend the Mountain of the Lord? A Biblical Theology of the Book of Leviticus*, New Studies in Biblical Theology (Downers Grove, IL: InterVarsity Press, 2015), 39–49.

We also find confirmation of Moses's connection between the priesthood of Adam and Aaron when we read Ezekiel 28. When Ezekiel issues an oracle of judgment against Tyre, he portrays the king in priestly garments. Listing the stones emblazoned on Aaron's robe to portray the prince of Tyre in priestly garb (v. 13; cf. Ex. 28:15–21), Ezekiel compares the fall of Tyre to the fall of Adam.

> Son of man, sing a lament for the king of Tyre, and say to him, "This is what the sovereign LORD says:
>
>> "You were the sealer of perfection,
>> full of wisdom, and perfect in beauty.
>> You were in Eden, the garden of God.
>> Every precious stone was your covering,
>> the ruby, topaz, and emerald,
>> the chrysolite, onyx, and jasper,
>> the sapphire, turquoise, and beryl;
>> your settings and mounts were made of gold.
>> On the day you were created they were prepared.
>> I placed you there with an anointed guardian cherub;
>> you were on the holy mountain of God;
>> you walked about amidst fiery stones.
>> You were blameless in your behavior from the day you
>>   were created,
>> until sin was discovered in you." (28:12–15 NET)

Unlike the ESV and NASB, which identify this glorious being as an angel (v. 14), the NET juxtaposes Adam and the cherub, which makes better sense of the surrounding context.[11] In Genesis 3, it is

---

11. Cf. William J. Dumbrell, "Genesis 2:1–17: A Foreshadowing of the New Creation," in *Biblical Theology: Retrospect and Prospect*, ed. Scott J. Hafemann (Downers Grove, IL: InterVarstiy Press, 2002), 61; Daniel I. Block, *Ezekiel 25–48*, New International Commentary on the Old Testament (Grand Rapids, MI: Eerdmans, 1998), 99–112, 117.

the man whom God removes from his holy mountain, just as Ezekiel 28:16 records:

> You sinned;
> so I defiled you and banished you from the mountain
>   of God—
> the guardian cherub expelled you from the midst of the
>   stones of fire. (NET)

As far as we know, it was only Adam and his posterity that God cut off from Eden. Job 1:6; 2:1 and 1 Kings 22:21–22 indicate angelic beings standing before God. By comparing the king of Tyre's judgment to Adam's, we find imagery that suggests how glorious Adam was and how far humankind fell. Created as a priest to rule over God's creation, humanity now suffers under God's curse in a world plagued by death—the very thing, because of its uncleanness, that priests were called to avoid (Lev. 21:1–4).

Last, Luke 3:38 bears witness to Adam's priesthood. When Luke traces Jesus's genealogy back to Adam, he calls Adam "the son of God." The priestly significance of this title is associated with the way firstborn sons were set apart as priestly assistants. As Michael Morales observes, firstborn sons were consecrated to the Lord (see Ex. 13:2), and until Numbers 3:40–51 replaced firstborn sons with the Levites, the firstborn sons "were to serve in a lay-priestly role."[12] And part of this connection between sonship and priesthood goes back to Adam.

In all, when we read Genesis with the rest of the Pentateuch, we find considerable evidence for seeing Adam as a priest. And in the rest of the Bible, we will continue to see how Adam's priesthood

---

12. L. Michael Morales, "The Levitical Priesthood," *Southern Baptist Journal of Theology* 23, no. 1 (2019): 8–12.

echoes through redemptive history until it finds its climax in Jesus Christ.

Echoes of Eden: Priesthood in the Patriarchs

If Genesis 1–3 gives evidence for Adam's priesthood, the rest of Genesis echoes his priesthood. Only now, because sin has torn asunder the covenant between God and man, the mediating role of priests will center on the offering of animal sacrifices. Similarly, because Genesis precedes the giving of the law, the priesthood that echoes among the patriarchs is not as clear as what will be revealed in the Sinai legislation. Nevertheless, in the patriarchs we find priestly echoes that range from priestly actions among various figures to one striking priest figure, Melchizedek, who is called the priest of God Most High.

Going back to our definition of priesthood,[13] we can see how the patriarchs are presented as priests in three primary ways: (1) serving at and/or sanctifying a holy place, (2) bringing a sacrifice to the altar, and (3) speaking to God for people (prayer) or speaking to others from God (blessings). With these priestly actions in mind, we find Abel, Seth, Noah, and Abraham doing priestly things (see table 1). Because these men are never called priests, we must be cautious about overstating their roles. Nevertheless, we should not ignore the way Moses presents their actions. In what follows, we will trace the echoes of priesthood through these four men, focusing most of our attention on Abraham, before coming to Melchizedek, the priest who stands out in Genesis and the rest of the Bible.[14]

---

13. Priests are consecrated mediators between God and his covenant people who stand to serve at God's altar (1) sanctifying God's Holy Place, (2) sacrificing God's offerings, and (3) speaking God's covenant.

14. Technically, Potiphera is another priest mentioned in Genesis (41:45, 50; 46:20), but his service in Egypt puts him beyond the scope of this study.

Table 1. Patriarchs as priests in three ways

Patriarchal Priests	Sanctifying a Place	Sacrificing at the Altar	Speaking the Word
Abel, Seth	The "door" of Eden (Gen. 4:7)	"Firstborn of the flock and of their fat portion" (Gen. 4:4) God desires a sin offering (Gen. 4:7; cf. 4:3, 8, 14).	With Seth, people call upon the name of the Lord (Gen. 4:26).
Noah	Altar (Gen. 8:20) "Clean animals" (Gen. 8:20)	"Burnt offerings" (Gen. 8:20) Sacrifices to please the Lord (Gen. 8:21)	Noah offers a blessing (Gen. 9:26).
Abraham (Isaac, Jacob)*	Altars (Gen. 12:7–8; 13:4, 18; cf. 26:25; 33:20) Mount Moriah (Gen. 22:2, 9), i.e., Jerusalem (2 Chron. 3:1)	Abraham offers a burnt offering (Gen. 22:2, 3, 6, 7, 8, 13). A lamb is provided in place of Isaac (Gen. 22:13–14).	Abraham and his sons mediate blessing (Gen. 12:1–3; 22:17–18; cf. 27:29; 48:15–20; 49:25–26).
Melchizedek	Salem (Gen. 14:18), i.e., Jerusalem (Ps. 76:2)	Bread and wine symbolize a covenant meal (Gen. 14:18).	Melchizedek speaks of God Most High (Gen. 14:18–19). Melchizedek blesses Abraham (Gen. 14:19–20).

* Like their father Abraham, both Isaac and Jacob build altars (Gen. 26:25; 33:20) and worship God as priests.

Abel and Seth. The first echo of priesthood is found in the accounts of Abel and Seth. For example, Moses juxtaposes the faithful sacrifice of Abel with the unacceptable sacrifice of Cain in Genesis 4:1–7.[15] In this contrast, we learn something about faith, worship, and sacrifice. Writing to a people who knew the Levitical system of sacrifice, Moses describes Israel's ancestors worshiping with terms taken from the law. Accordingly, Adam's sons offer sacrifices at "the original sanctuary door, the gate of Eden guarded by cherubim," just like

---

15. A more thorough study could consider the faulty priesthood of Cain and others. For brevity's sake, this chapter will only consider the faithful sons of Adam.

Israelites would bring their sacrifices to the "entrance of the tent of meeting" (e.g., Lev. 1:3, 5; 3:2).[16] In this context, Abel proves his faith by offering the "firstborn of his flock" (Gen. 4:4). Cain's offering, by contrast, displeases God because his unacceptable sacrifice indicates a deficiency in both his heart (cf. 1 John 3:12) and his sacrifice.[17] As William Symington once observed, "Had Cain possessed Abel's faith, he would have presented Abel's sacrifice," but instead Cain "trusted to [*sic*] his own merit for acceptance," thus sealing God's displeasure with his offering and highlighting the faith required to approach God (cf. Heb. 11:4).[18]

Seth also demonstrates his priestly faith when he and the people "began to call upon the name of the LORD" (Gen. 4:26). As Scripture testifies later, calling upon the Lord reflects praise and prayer (Ps. 116:13, 17),[19] but it also describes the priestly actions of Samuel, Aaron, and Moses. Psalm 99:6 states,

> Moses and Aaron were among his priests,
>> Samuel also was among those who *called upon his name*.
>> They called to the LORD, and he answered them.

In these two examples, the priestly duties of Abel and Seth are faint. Yet the pattern of priesthood is seen in their composite: together they (1) have a holy place, (2) bring an acceptable sacrifice, and (3) "call upon . . . the LORD" in prayer. These actions suggest that these sons of Adam are priestly servants of God, servants whose priesthood will be magnified in the life of Noah.

---

16. Morales, *Who Shall Ascend?*, 57. Morales goes on to argue persuasively that Gen. 4:7 should be translated as "'a sin offering lies at the door/entrance [*petah*]' (rather than 'sin crouches at the door', as in the door of Cain's heart or tent)."

17. William Symington, *On the Atonement and Intercession of Jesus Christ* (Pittsburgh, PA: United Presbyterian Board of Publication, 1864), 66–92, esp. 80–83.

18. Symington, *The Atonement and Intercession of Jesus*, 83.

19. See Graeme Goldsworthy, *Prayer and the Knowledge of God: What the Whole Bible Teaches* (Downers Grove, IL: InterVarsity Press, 2003), 72, 110–11.

Noah. Noah's story is well known, but his priesthood less so. When we stand Noah next to Adam, however, we begin see how Moses presents him as a priest. Likewise, when we read his story in light of the Levitical priests, we also see how Noah exhibits priestly actions.

First, Noah builds the first altar in the Bible (Gen. 8:20). In Scripture, altars are the designated "place [for] slaughtering the sacrifice."[20] In time, altars become the place where priests apply the blood of the offering. As Leviticus 1–7 makes clear, it is not the sacrifice that makes someone a priest; it is the application of the blood to the altar. Before the law appoints Aaron and his sons to serve at the altar, Abraham, Isaac, and Jacob all build altars to offer sacrifices (Gen. 12:7–8; 13:4, 18; 22:9; 26:25; 33:20; 35:1, 3, 7). Following the pattern of priesthood, this announcement that Noah builds an altar speaks to his priestly calling.

Next, the words used to describe Noah's sacrifice in Genesis 8:20–21—"clean," "burnt offerings," "pleasing aroma"—are all Levitical (i.e., from the priestly book of Leviticus). Identifying the type of Noah's offering is tempting but such a connection may not be possible. Noah makes a sacrifice without a full knowledge of Moses's law. Nevertheless, Moses's language suggests that Noah's sacrifice is "a prototype of the work of later priests who made atonement for Israel."[21] Certainly, it furthers expectations for a priesthood that is to come.

Third, Noah mediates a covenant with creation. Yahweh states in Genesis 9:9–10, "I establish my covenant with you *and your offspring after you, and with every living creature that is with you.*" In these

---

20. Allen P. Ross, *Recalling the Hope of Glory: Biblical Worship from the Garden to the New Creation* (Grand Rapids, MI: Kregel Academic, 2006), 138; cf. Tremper Longman III, *Immanuel in Our Place: Seeing Christ in Israel's Worship*, The Gospel according to the Old Testament (Phillipsburg, NJ: P&R, 2001), 15–16.

21. Gordon J. Wenham, "The Theology of Old Testament Sacrifice," in *Sacrifice in the Bible*, ed. Roger T. Beckwith and Martin J. Selman (Grand Rapids, MI: Baker, 1995; repr., Eugene, OR: Wipf & Stock, 2004), 80.

verses, Yahweh identifies Noah as the individual through whom he will preserve the world.[22] Like Adam's, Noah's mediating role between God and man identifies his priestly vocation. In the rest of the Bible, priests play a significant role in maintaining God's covenants, and so it is here. Even more, Noah speaks the word of God's blessing to Shem and Japheth (Gen. 9:26–27). In this blessing, we find another mark of his priesthood—namely, speech that communicates God's blessing. Later, it will be the Levitical priests who bless God's people (cf. Num. 6:24–26) and pronounce blessings and curses (Deut. 27:9–10; Josh. 8:33).[23]

In sum, Noah's actions (e.g., building an altar, offering a clean sacrifice, mediating a covenant, and pronouncing a blessing) highlight his priestly service and add another layer to the story of priesthood developing in Scripture. Still, his priesthood remains faint, especially as we come to Abraham.

Abraham. After the people of Shinar attempt to build a tower into the heavens (Gen. 11:1–9), the account of Genesis turns to Abram (later renamed Abraham). Elected by God to be the recipient and conduit of blessing to all the families of the earth (12:1–3), Abraham is a central figure in redemptive history. Like Noah's, his priestly identity is found in (1) the altars he builds, (2) the intercession he makes, and (3) the sacrifice he offers on Mount Moriah.[24] From these three actions, we see the pattern of priesthood in Abraham's life. Yet the most compelling reason to see Abraham's priestly status is his relationship to Melchizedek, the priest-king from Salem. From these

---

22. Genesis 9 goes on to explain the covenant of common grace. Noah's covenant promises universal preservation, not eternal salvation.

23. Richard D. Nelson, *Raising Up a Faithful Priest: Community and Priesthood in Biblical Theology* (Louisville: Westminster John Knox, 1993), 44–46.

24. I have argued at length for this in "Restoring the Image of God: A Corporate-Filial Approach to the 'Royal Priesthood' in Exodus 19:6," *Southern Baptist Journal of Theology* 22, no. 2 (2018): 37–41.

four lines of evidence, we will see how Moses describes Abraham in priestly terms.

First, Abraham builds altars to worship God. Actually, he builds three altars (Gen. 12:7–9; 13:18) before he builds the climactic altar on Mount Moriah where God provides a ram in place of Isaac (Gen. 22:9). Each of these altars is a place of worship, which harkens back to Eden and Adam's role as priest. As Peter Gentry and Stephen Wellum note, "Canaan is depicted in Edenic language as a mountain sanctuary," and Abraham is the one "fulfilling an Adamic role, [as] he offers sacrifice as a priest and worships God in this mountain sanctuary."[25] While Moses takes little time to explain these altars, they identify Abraham as a priest in his own day.

Second, Abraham's intercession before God points to his priesthood. Yahweh tells Abraham of his plan to destroy Sodom because of its wickedness (Gen. 18). In response, Abraham pleads for God to spare the righteous, making multiple petitions for God's mercy (vv. 22–33). Of note, the language of these verses—"*stood* before the Lord" (v. 22) and "*drew near*" (v. 24)—are often used of priests.[26] Moreover, Genesis 19:29 explains why God spares Lot: "When God destroyed the cities of the valley [Sodom and Gomorrah], God remembered Abraham and sent Lot out of the midst of the overthrow when he overthrew the cities in which Lot had lived." Whether this rescue is a direct result of Abraham's efficacious prayer or more generally from the blessing God would bestow on those in Abraham's family (Gen. 12:3), Lot is delivered because God remembers Abraham. Throughout the Bible, priests take up this position of mediating between God and man, and in Abraham we see the same.

---

25. Gentry and Wellum, *Kingdom through Covenant*, 235. Cf. T. Desmond Alexander, *From Eden to the New Jerusalem: An Introduction to Biblical Theology* (Grand Rapids, MI: Kregel, 2008), 83.

26. Peter J. Leithart, *The Priesthood of the Plebs: A Theology of Baptism* (Eugene, OR: Wipf & Stock, 2003), 64–71.

Admittedly, prophets also play a role in covenant mediation and intercessory prayer. Abraham is called a "prophet" when asked to intercede for Abimelech in Genesis 20:7. This might suggest Abraham is a prophet only, and not a priest. Yet this would miss three points. First, the fact that prophets intercede for others does not deny the essentially priestly nature of prayer (cf. Gen. 4:26; Ps. 99:6). In fact, God often resorts to sending prophets to Israel when the priests fail to fulfill their ministry of teaching and intercession. Second, many Old Testament prophets are also identified as priests (e.g., Moses, Samuel, Jeremiah, Ezekiel). Thus, there can be some overlap between the offices and their respective assignments. Third and most importantly, the point is not that intercessory prayer is *sufficient* to make one a priest but that it is *necessary*.

Third, Abraham's priestly duties are evidenced in his (near) sacrifice of Isaac. In Genesis 22 we find three reasons why Abraham's sacrifice is priestly. First, the location of the offering on Mount Moriah is associated with priestly sacrifices (vv. 2, 14). Second Chronicles 3:1 indicates Solomon's temple was built on this mountaintop, which David purchased from Araunah to offer sacrifices for his own sin (2 Sam. 24:18–25). Not only does the shared location of these altars prefigure the location of Christ's sacrifice (on a hill outside the city of Jerusalem), but if "Salem" in Genesis 14:18 is Jerusalem, as Psalm 76:2 suggests, then Abraham would be returning to the mountain of Melchizedek in order to offer his priestly sacrifice of his beloved son. We will consider the priestly connections between Abraham and Melchizedek shortly.

A second reason why Abraham's sacrifice is priestly is that some of the language of Genesis 22 suggests a priestly sacrifice. For instance, Abraham says that his three-day journey to the mountain of the Lord will result in "worship." Likewise, Moses uses the word "burnt offering" six times to speak of Isaac's sacrifice (vv. 2, 3, 6,

7, 8, 13). In Genesis, "burnt offering" is only used of Noah's sacrifice (8:20) before it is used in Exodus–Deuteronomy to speak of tabernacle sacrifices. Moreover, Yahweh's provision of a sacrifice on Mount Moriah (22:13–14) foreshadows the provision of sacrificial lambs that would redeem the firstborn of Israel in the Passover and comprise the heart of worship in Leviticus.

The third reason is that Abraham's obedience to the Lord at the expense of his family is unmistakably priestly. In obedience to God, he does not raise his knife as bloodthirsty father; he does so as a loyal, God-appointed priest. That Abraham functions as a priest is evident from applying Deuteronomy 33:9 to Abraham. Whereas this verse would explain why the priests and Levites were called to serve at the Lord's house, it could be applied to Abraham: "[Abraham] disowned his brothers and ignored his children. For [he] observed your word and kept your covenant." In Exodus 32:25–29, God ordains the Levites to be a priestly tribe because of their allegiance to God *against* their kinsman. So here we find that Abraham, Levi's ancestor, is equally faithful to God as he secures the blessing by his sacrificial obedience (Gen. 22:18; 26:5).

Truly, faithfulness of this kind is what secures the place of the Levites to serve in God's tabernacle (Deut. 33:9–10). Likewise, priestly faithfulness is what secures the covenant with Levi in Numbers 25. As we will come to see, God's priests are chosen by God (as Abraham is) and prove their faithfulness by doing all they are commanded at God's altar (as Abraham does). In his testing (Gen. 22:1), therefore, Abraham proves himself to be a faithful priest and one whose actions bring blessing to others.

In these three ways, we find solid evidence for identifying Abraham's actions as priestly. Yet Abraham's priestly identification is further clarified through his connection to Melchizedek, the king of Salem, who is priest of God Most High. Though enigmatic in himself, this mysterious figure will become the most important priest in the Bible—or at least, the most important until another comes in his priestly order (Heb. 7:11). In Genesis, it is Abraham's interaction with Melchizedek that both confirms his own priestly identity and sets up a priestly expectation that will take the rest of the Bible to reveal.

The Enigma of the Priesthood: A Priest Like Melchizedek

In Genesis 14:18 Moses identifies Melchizedek as the king of Salem and priest of God Most High. This royal priest shows up *by name* only three times in the Bible (Gen. 14; Ps. 110; Hebrews), but his appearances mark some of the most significant developments in redemptive history. Because this historical figure plays such an important part in understanding the royal priesthood of Jesus, I will include the full text:

> After his return from the defeat of Chedorlaomer and the kings who were with him, the king of Sodom went out to meet him at the Valley of Shaveh (that is, the King's Valley). And Melchizedek king of Salem brought out bread and wine. (He was priest of God Most High.) And he blessed him and said,
>
> > "Blessed be Abram by God Most High,
> >   Possessor of heaven and earth;
> > and blessed be God Most High,
> >   who has delivered your enemies into your hand!"

And Abram gave him a tenth of everything. And the king of Sodom said to Abram, "Give me the persons, but take the goods for yourself." But Abram said to the king of Sodom, "I have lifted my hand to the LORD, God Most High, Possessor of heaven and earth, that I would not take a thread or a sandal strap or anything that is yours, lest you should say, 'I have made Abram rich.' I will take nothing but what the young men have eaten, and the share of the men who went with me. Let Aner, Eshcol, and Mamre take their share." (Gen. 14:17–24)

In these eight verses, we find Abraham returning from battle, where he has defeated the armies of Canaan (v. 17). On his return, Abraham encounters two kings who "represent two different kinds of kingship."[27] Discerning the difference, Abraham rejects the offer of Sodom's king ("Give me the persons, but take the goods for yourself") and honors voluntarily Salem's king. Though Genesis 14:1–16 presents Abraham as greater than all the kings in Canaan, his tithe to Melchizedek evidences Abraham's acknowledgment that Melchizedek is a greater priest-king.

As Hebrews 7 will show us, every feature of Genesis 14 is valuable for interpretation. For our purposes, it is illuminating that he is a king of *righteousness* ("Melchizedek" means "king of righteousness" in Hebrew) and a king of *peace* ("Salem" is a variation of the Hebrew word for "peace"). Likewise, he is a priest of the Most High God (v. 18). In Genesis 14, Abraham recognizes Melchizedek's greatness (Heb. 7:7). First, he honors him by receiving Melchizedek's bread and wine and eating a meal with this royal priest. Next, he joins in blessing Melchizedek's God Most High (Gen. 14:22). And last, by returning a tithe to Melchizedek from the spoils of war (Gen. 14:20), he acknowledges Melchizedek as superior to himself. In this exchange, Melchizedek provides a glimpse of what Adam might have been, what Israel was meant to be(come), and what Jesus Christ would ultimately be—a glorious royal priest.

---

27. Gentry and Wellum, *Kingdom through Covenant*, 237.

Yet the reader of Genesis does not have to wait until the New Testament to see a righteous royal priest. Rather, by keeping our finger on the text, we see in the next chapter how Abraham is declared "righteous" when he believes God (Gen. 15:6). Then, in Genesis 17:6, 16, Yahweh promises Abraham that royal sons will come from his line. And finally, in Genesis 22, Abraham brings a sacrifice to the altar on Mount Moriah, the hill associated with Melchizedek, the one that David will later claim by means of his own costly sacrifice (2 Sam. 24:24–25). Read together, Abraham's righteousness, the promise of royal sons, and the presentation of a priestly sacrifice identify Abraham as a royal priest like Melchizedek.

Indeed, while Melchizedek disappears from the pages of Scripture after Genesis 14 (until Ps. 110), his shadow remains. In Abraham and his offspring, the combination of righteousness, priesthood, and kingship will be passed down from generation to generation, until the seed of Abraham (Gal. 3:16) becomes the priest-king like Melchizedek. Therefore, we find in the annals of Israel's history the hope of a royal priest who will surpass all others.

In some ways, this hope will be realized at Sinai, when Israel as God's son (Ex. 4:22–23) will be called a "kingdom of priests" (Ex. 19:6). In other ways, David will take up the mantle of being a priestly king like Melchizedek when he brings the ark of the covenant to Jerusalem. Still, the ultimate fulfillment of Melchizedek's legacy will be the son of Abraham and the son of David (Matt. 1:1), Jesus Christ, who will prove to be the superlative royal priest.

In all these ways, Genesis gives us a pattern of priesthood. In Adam, we find the evidence of the first priest; in the patriarchs, especially Abraham, we find echoes of Adam's priesthood and anticipations of a greater priest to come. Finally, in Melchizedek we find an enigmatic figure that stands out among all the other patriarchal priests. By his interaction with Abraham, we begin to see how this royal priest of Salem enters the story of the priesthood, but we will have to wait until Psalm 110 and the New Testament before we understand his role completely.

For now, we need to see how this original pattern of priesthood is formalized in the law. Indeed, what comes next is the legislation of the pattern and the narrowing of the priesthood from all of Abraham's offspring to one tribe in Israel. Indeed, the union of priesthood and kingship will soon be legally divided, but not forever—only until a righteous son of Abraham will come to be a royal priest after the order of Melchizedek.

2

The Law

The Levitical Priesthood Legislated

In Dearborn, Michigan, there is a historic site called Greenfield Village, established by Henry Ford. More than a hundred buildings capture the spirit and story of the industrial revolution. Included in this living museum is a steam locomotive. At the locomotive's wheelhouse stands a diagram displaying how the engine works. Through a series of visual images, visitors can see how the coal burns to make steam, the steam creates pressure to turn the pistons, and the pistons power the massive train down the tracks. This technology no longer serves our country, but there is something instructive in learning how this now obsolete system worked.

Similarly, when we look into the priestly system of the old covenant, we discover a system of mediation no longer in effect. At first, this might make us wonder what good it is to study the intricacies of the law. Yet, as we will see in this chapter, it is only as we look to

Israel's cultic system (i.e., the tabernacle, the sacrifices, and especially the priests and Levites) that we find a visual aid for learning how God desires to be worshiped. Indeed, the "pattern" of worship revealed at Sinai (see Ex. 25:9, 40) gave Moses a look into heaven, and today it provides the church with a pattern for new covenant worship.

Like the diagram displaying ancient engines for modern travelers to better appreciate how people got around in the past, the Levitical priesthood helps us better understand what it means to be priests in God's kingdom. While full comprehension of this priestly glory awaits the New Testament, the law of Moses prefigures Christ and the kingdom of priests he is gathering. Therefore, as we open the Pentateuch (Moses's five books), we will learn more fully what priesthood means and how its ancient legislation prepares for Christ and his church.

In this chapter, we follow three steps. First, we will watch how the priesthood develops under the ministry of Moses. Because the term "Levitical priesthood" is not formalized until Deuteronomy, it is important to see how a series of events, beginning in Exodus and continuing through Numbers, forms a multilayered system of priestly mediation. The Levitical priesthood is the culmination of Yahweh calling Aaron and his sons to serve as priests and then adding "priestly personnel" from the house of Levi (the Levites) to strengthen this priestly arrangement.[1]

Second, we will consider what the priests and Levites do in and around God's tabernacle (see table 2). Synthesizing the complex details of the law into five aspects of priesthood, we will see how Aaron and his sons (1) mediate the covenant, (2) guard the tabernacle, (3) bring sacrifices to the altar, (4) teach the people, and (5) intercede

---

1. "Levitical priests" is found only in Deut. 17:9, 18; 18:1; 24:8; 27:9.

for Israel. We will also see what the Levites do to assist their brothers, observing the distinction that Levites are priestly assistants.

Table 2. The cultic system in Israel*

Tabernacle/Temple	Priest(s)	Sacrifice(s)
The Holy Place God chose to dwell on earth with his covenant people	The consecrated mediator(s) between God and his covenant people who stand to serve at God's altar (1) sanctifying God's Holy Place, (2) sacrificing God's offerings, (3) speaking God's covenant†	The substitutionary system of covenant sacrifice provided by God for the pardoning of sin and cleansing of impurity

* Though our modern minds may define "cult" as a heretical sect, in the Bible "cult" is shorthand for a system of worship with three constituent parts: (1) a sacred place, (2) a sacred personnel, and (3) a sacred system of sacrifice.

† On various definitions of priesthood, see Peter J. Leithart, "Attendants of Yahweh's House: Priesthood in the Old Testament," *Journal for the Study of the Old Testament* 85 (1999): 3–24. My definition combines his emphasis on standing in the temple to serve with the actions of the priests—namely, guarding God's place, sacrificing God's offerings, and teaching God's people.

Third, we will see how a greater priest is needed. For all that the law instructs concerning priests and Levites, it is still a system of mediation weakened by sin and death. In succession, Israel, Aaron, the Levites, and Moses all fail to live up to their "priestly" callings. Accordingly, we will see in the Pentateuch itself what Hebrews declares later, that the Levitical priesthood was incapable of bringing eternal redemption. Thus, while giving us God's authorized pattern for priesthood, the law of Moses anticipates the need for a greater priesthood. Yet we cannot understand that later priesthood without understanding the priesthood legislated in Israel.

The Storyline of Priesthood in Israel

As we saw in the last chapter, the first person identified as a "priest" in the Bible is Melchizedek (Gen. 14:18). The second priest is Potiphera, Joseph's father-in-law (Gen. 41:45, 50; 46:20), and the third is Jethro,

Moses's father-in-law (Ex. 2:16; 3:1; 18:1). Still, as it relates to Israel's priesthood, we must look to Aaron and the tribe of Levi. For these other priests reinforce the point that priesthood is common among Israel's neighbors, but they do not contribute to Israel's priesthood.[2]

According to Moses's five books, no single passage establishes the priesthood in Israel. Rather, a series of events results in the Levitical priesthood. By my count, there are at least twelve "chapters" worth mentioning in this story. I will mention the places that contribute to the priesthood in Israel like milestones on a scenic journey. Space precludes a detailed investigation of each chapter, but I will attempt to highlight the key ideas, so that interested readers can study these passages on their own.[3]

First, Israel is identified as a kingdom of priests. When the Lord delivers Israel from Egypt, he brings them to his holy mountain. At Mount Sinai, Yahweh makes a covenant with Israel and declares that Israel is to be a royal priesthood or kingdom of priests. Exodus 19:5–6 reads, "Now therefore, if you will indeed obey my voice and keep my covenant, you shall be my treasured possession among all peoples, for all the earth is mine; and you shall be to me a kingdom of priests and a holy nation."

This priestly calling sets Israel apart from the other nations. It does not mean Israel is the only nation with priests, but it does mean Israel is God's chosen priesthood. At Sinai, Yahweh gives his covenant partner his law and a pattern for worship. At the center of this worship are priests who stand to serve in God's house. These priests will model the kind of holy service God expects

---

2. Interestingly, the first three priests named in Scripture are all Gentiles. And at least two of them, Melchizedek and Jethro, appear to worship (or come to worship, in the case of Jethro) the true God of heaven.

3. For a more detailed history of this development, see my "How a Kingdom of Priests Became a Kingdom with Priests and Levites: A Filial-Corporate Understanding of the Royal Priesthood in Exodus 19:6," *Southern Baptist Journal of Theology* 23, no. 1 (2019): 23–56.

from Israel, a nation of people called to adorn themselves with holiness.

Second, Israel's firstborn sons serve as priestly assistants. In the Passover, Exodus 13:2 states, firstborn sons are set apart for the Lord. Yahweh commands: "Consecrate to me all the firstborn. Whatever is the first to open the womb among the people of Israel, both of man and of beast, is mine." A few verses later, Exodus 13:13 requires future firstborns to be redeemed. We will see *how* this works when we consider the Levites in Numbers 3. For now, it is important to see how Israel's *national* priesthood relates to Israelites *individually*.

For starters, every father acts like a priest during the Passover, when fathers apply the blood of a sacrificed lamb to the lintel and doorposts of their homes (Ex. 12:23). This blood is the way God spares firstborn sons in Israel and causes Pharaoh to set God's firstborn (the nation of Israel) free (Ex. 4:22–23). Memorializing this event and the purchase of firstborn sons for holy service, Exodus 13 calls future generations to redeem their firstborn sons, who are consecrated unto the Lord. The reasoning for this consecration can be seen in the way Israel will keep covenant with God. Just as the priests will be set apart to lead the nation to keep covenant with Yahweh, so firstborn sons are to help their fathers lead their families to do the same. Put differently, just as Israel (as God's firstborn) becomes a kingdom of priests when God enters into covenant at Sinai, so God intends for Israel's firstborn sons to have priestly responsibilities within the people he is bringing into the land.

The evidence for firstborn sons serving as priestly assistants can be seen at Sinai. In Exodus 19 "priests" are called to consecrate themselves (v. 22) and to help keep the people from ascending the mountain (v. 24). Similarly, in Exodus 24:5, we find Moses instructing "young men" to go to the people on behalf of Moses. These young men are described as those "who offered burnt offerings and sacrificed peace offerings of oxen to the LORD." Commenting on the identity of these priests, Walter Kaiser observes that these assistants "must be a reference to the 'firstborn' of every family who were dedicated and consecrated to God ([Ex.] 13:2). Only later was the tribe of Levi substituted for each firstborn male (Num. 3:45)."[4] Indeed, from what we saw in Genesis, it is very likely that the sons of Israel assist Moses at Sinai, before the law identifies Aaron and his sons to be the priests.

Though details of this point may seem superfluous at first, we will find that the consecration of the firstborn (Ex. 13:2; cf. Num. 3:13) is quoted in Luke 2:23 to explain Jesus's dedication at the temple. The New Testament makes many connections between Jesus's status as God's firstborn son and his priestly service. And thus, it is valuable to see how priestly service goes from firstborn sons to the house of Levi under the direction of the law. It will not be surprising that when the law is fulfilled by Christ, the priesthood will return to God's firstborn son and all those who find their priestly status in union with him.

Third, Aaron and his sons are chosen as priests. When Moses receives a pattern of the tabernacle in Exodus 25–31, it comes complete with instructions for priests. In particular, God chooses Aaron and his sons as the priests who will stand at the altar and serve in his house. Because we will consider the duties of priests below, my comments here can be brief.

As noted in the previous chapter, Adam is presented as a royal priest created to serve in God's garden sanctuary. Though

---

4. Walter Kaiser, "Exodus," in *The Expositor's Bible Commentary*, ed. Frank E. Gaebelein, vol. 2 (Grand Rapids, MI: Zondervan, 1990), 419.

unclothed, Adam was created to reflect the glory of his Maker. Psalm 8 even speaks of Adam being crowned with glory and honor. When Adam disobeyed God's word, he failed in his priestly duty to guard the garden from the serpent. Now, in the tabernacle, for the first time since God expelled Adam from his holy mountain (cf. Ezek. 28:16), God is clothing a man with "glory" and "beauty" (Ex. 28:2, 40) and inviting him to draw near. The visual symbols of Aaron's garments connect him to Adam. For instance, Aaron's clothing reflects the glory of God's house and the position of a temple servant. Likewise, the gold and jewels are reflective of the precious metals of Eden (see Gen. 2:11–12). Moreover, as the mediating figure between God and God's kingdom, Aaron, like Adam, will be the source of blessing to God's people. In the other direction, because Aaron's breastpiece carries the names of the twelve tribes on his clothing, Aaron brings the people of Israel before the Lord whenever he serves at the altar.[5]

Unfortunately, Aaron will also fail to live up to his glorious calling, just like Adam. In Exodus 32, Aaron fashions a golden calf and leads the people to worship God falsely. As the story of the priesthood develops, this event will have significance in multiple directions. For instance, it calls for Moses to intercede for Aaron (Deut. 9:20), and it requires the Levites to replace Israel's firstborn sons as assistants to the priests (Num. 3:40–51). These are the next two chapters in the story.

Fourth, Moses serves as a priest. In the Pentateuch, Moses never calls himself a priest. Yet, as we have learned, priests can be observed by their actions. With that in mind, we can see that in building altars (Ex. 17:15; 24:4), bringing sacrifices to the altar (Ex. 24:6), and

---

5. For more on the relationship between Aaron and Adam, see Michael Morales, *Who Shall Ascend the Mountain of the Lord? A Biblical Theology of the Book of Leviticus*, New Studies in Biblical Theology (Downers Grove, IL: InterVarsity Press, 2015), 39–49.

delivering Yahweh's covenant to the people of Israel, Moses is acting like a priest.

Still, it is not the accumulation of these actions alone that should get our greatest attention. Rather, it is Moses's role as intercessor. Among Moses's many priestly actions, intercession for Israel *and* Aaron stands at the center. Without Moses's intercession, the whole project of the tabernacle might not have continued. In Exodus 32, Aaron follows the lead of the people and makes a golden calf. This act of rebellion not only breaks the covenant but also jeopardizes his own priesthood. In response to this transgression, Moses intercedes for Israel four times (32:11–13, 31–32; 33:12–18; 34:9). Deuteronomy 9:20 reveals that Moses also prays for Aaron, pleading God's mercy to fall on this erring priest. Through his priestly intercession, we see Moses call upon the Lord, which is what Psalm 99:6 cites when it labels Moses a priest.

Exodus 32–34 shows how Yahweh, in response to Moses's intercession, relents from his judgment, discloses his steadfast love and faithfulness, permits Aaron to continue as priest, reestablishes the covenant, and enables the tabernacle to be built. In this way, the pattern of worship revealed at Sinai not only comes through Moses as a covenant mediator; it also comes through his priestly prayer. In fact, it would not be too much to say that in interceding for Aaron, Moses proves himself to be a greater priest than Aaron.

Fifth, the firstborn sons of Israel are replaced with the Levites. As observed above, firstborn sons were set apart for service to the Lord when God redeemed the firstborn sons in the Passover. However, the service of the firstborn would come to an abrupt end when Israel worshiped the golden calf. Numbers 3 describes the substitution of Levites for firstborn sons, and Deuteronomy 33:9 commends the loyalty of Levites to stand with the Lord. However, it is Exodus 32:25–29 that describes the historical event that brought forth the need for Levites to redeem the firstborn sons of Israel.

In Exodus 32, when Moses sees Israel's idolatry (v. 25), he issues a question and a command: "Who is on the LORD's side? Come to me" (v. 26). Significantly, *only* and *all* the Levites come. Verse 29 states, "Today you have been ordained for the service of the LORD, each one at the cost of his son and of his brother, so that he might bestow a blessing upon you this day." The "cost of his son and of his brother" is explained by verses 27–28:

> And he said to them, "Thus says the LORD God of Israel, 'Put your sword on your side each of you, and go to and fro from gate to gate throughout the camp, and each of you kill his brother and his companion and his neighbor.'" And the sons of Levi did according to the word of Moses. And that day about three thousand men of the people fell.

Unlike Adam, who failed to take God's side when Eve sinned, these Levites prove themselves faithful as they turn against their kinsmen (cf. Deut. 33:9). God recognizes their loyalty and assigns them the task of guarding his house and serving their brothers, the priests. We will consider the Levites' duties below, but first we need to see how the entire book of Leviticus instructs Aaron and his sons.

Sixth, the priests are given instructions for the house of God. Leviticus, as it is called in our English Bibles,[6] reveals how God's dwelling place can be(come) a tent of meeting.[7] In its twenty-seven chapters, we find a priestly manual for the sons of Aaron. And in this stage of

---

6. The title Leviticus ("relating to the Levites") is something of a misnomer. The Hebrew title is "and he called" (see Lev. 1:1). More appropriately, Leviticus might be called "instruction for the priests," as the Mishnah has it. As we will see, the Levites are mentioned in only one passage (Lev. 25:32–33), which indicates this book is written for the sons of Aaron more than the Levites in general.

7. Morales, *Who Shall Ascend?*, 109–22.

development, we need to consider whom this book is for and what this book is about.

First, the book of Leviticus is ironically not for the Levites. In the Pentateuch, and throughout the Bible, "priest" is not synonymous with Levite. In fact, Levites are only mentioned four times in Leviticus (25:32–33). Instead, Leviticus is a book of instructions for the priests, who are the sons of Aaron. As we discovered from Exodus 28–29, God has called Aaron and his sons to serve at the altar. Levites stand on the perimeter of God's house, but they cannot approach the altar or the holy precincts within the tabernacle. The high priest, the priests, and the Levites correspond to different levels of holiness in and around God's house. We will return to these various levels of holiness below.

For now, we must see what Leviticus *is* about. And perhaps the best way to understand Leviticus is by seeing its outline. By observing the arrangement of the book (fig. 2), we can see what is central and how the whole book moves toward the house of God on the Day of Atonement (Lev. 1–16). From there the book returns to the people of God (Lev. 17–27), including the promise that God will walk among his people (26:12–13).

Figure 2. The priestly center of the Pentateuch*

Leviticus 1–7—Sacrifices

    Leviticus 8–10—Institution of priesthood, inauguration
        of cultus

        Leviticus 11–15—Clean versus unclean in daily life

            Leviticus 16—Day of Atonement

        Leviticus 17–20—Holy versus profane in daily life

    Leviticus 21–22—Legislation for the priesthood

Leviticus 23–27—Festivals, sacred times

* This figure approximates a diagram in Morales, *Who Shall Ascend?*, 29.

Written while Israel camped at Sinai, Leviticus is a manual for priestly service. From the sacrifices that begin the book (Lev. 1–7) to the covenantal blessings that depend upon them (Lev. 26–27), priests play a central role in making God's house a holy dwelling where Israel can enjoy God's presence through a system of priestly mediation. In Leviticus we also find instructions for installing Aaron's sons for service (Lev. 8–9), regulations for how priests remain holy (Lev. 21–22), and instructions for the priests to give the people (Lev. 11–15; 17–20). Above all of these instructions, however, Moses gives intricate details for how the high priest is to make yearly purification for the Most Holy Place on the Day of Atonement (Lev. 16).

In this central chapter, Moses explains how the chief son of Aaron is to enter Yahweh's house to cleanse it from the polluting effects of sin. This act of purification ensures that all the other parts of the sacrificial system will work. In the daily offerings (Num. 28), the yearly festivals (Lev. 23), and the as-needed sacrifices (Lev. 1–7), God's altar and God's house are kept pure by the high priest's service on the Day of Atonement.[8] From this central Day of Atonement, the priests then make sure Israel can rightly approach the God who dwells in their midst. This is done through their ministry of teaching (Lev. 10:11) and through the assistance of Levites, which comes next in Numbers.

Seventh, the Levites are given to the priests. In Numbers God gives the Levites to the sons of Aaron. They are to assist the priests and guard them, even as they help transport and protect the house of God when it is erected. Accordingly, Numbers 3 spends ample time placing the Levites and priests around the tabernacle. By observing their positions (see fig. 3) we learn much about their roles of service.

---

8. In truth, all aspects of Leviticus are needed to keep the sacrificial system in order. However, the Day of Atonement's focus on the mercy seat of God is unique, as it cleanses God's throne. All other sacrifices purify the people.

Figure 3. Israel in camp

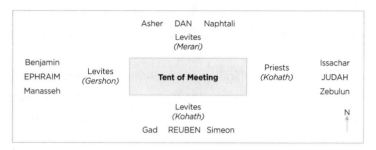

From this visual representation, we see the priests (the sons of Aaron) stand at the gate, while the three clans of Levi (Merari, Kohath, and Gershon) stand around the perimeter. In this arrangement, the Levites function as a security detail separating the priests and the people.[9] Numbers records Levi's invitation to serve and guard at the edge of God's holy precincts:

> Bring the tribe of Levi near, and set them before Aaron the priest, that they may minister to him. They shall keep guard over him and over the whole congregation before the tent of meeting, as they minister at the tabernacle. They shall guard all the furnishings of the tent of meeting, and keep guard over the people of Israel as they minister at the tabernacle. (3:6–8)

Numbers 3:9 also says the Levites are "given" to Aaron (cf. Num. 8:16, 19; 18:6–8). This means that the Levites are not priests unto themselves; they are priestly assistants who guard their brothers and serve at God's house. In this secondary role, the sons of Levi do not bring sacrifices to the altar. This point will be painfully reinforced when Korah (a son of Levi) attempts to make himself a priest like Aaron and Moses.

---

9. It is the unrestricted access of the people to Aaron that tempts this priest to make a golden calf (see Ex. 32:1–6).

At the end of Numbers 3, we also find how the Levites replace Israel's firstborn sons. This passage completes what we observed in Exodus 32. In this redemption, we discover an ongoing practice in Israel where firstborn sons are "redeemed" by a five-shekel offering. This gift provides for the priests and Levites serving in the tabernacle (cf. Ex. 30:11–16). But more than just a source of income, this perpetual "redemption price" reflects the way Levites serve in God's house in the place of Israel's firstborn sons. Understanding this practice is vital for recognizing the way Jesus would be presented at the temple in Luke 2:23. Strikingly, he would not be redeemed by a Levite; he would be presented as a true firstborn son dedicated to the Lord for service in God's house. Such an understanding of the priests and Levites is helpful because it furnishes us with information needed to make sense of Jesus's priesthood.

Eighth, the Levites are denied access to the altar. In Numbers 16 Korah, a Levite from the clan of Kohath, protests the priesthood of Aaron and Moses. Leading a band of 250 men, he argues that all in the assembly of Israel are holy; therefore, Aaron and Moses do not deserve special status (v. 3). Without defending himself directly, Moses exposes Korah's selfish ambition (vv. 8–11) and his illicit desire for the priesthood. Moses says to Korah in verse 10, "Would you seek the priesthood also?" Because of their vain ambition, Korah and his followers suffer an inglorious death—the earth swallows him, and fire consumes the 250 (vv. 31–35).

God's judgment reinforces the point—Levites are not priests, and priests cannot volunteer for the position; they must be chosen by God (see Ex. 28:1). Numbers 18 will clarify further: Levites are to assist Aaron's priesthood; they are not to approach the altar. In short, we can conclude from Numbers 16–18 that all priests are Levites, but not all Levites are priests. And so, when Deuteronomy speaks of the "Levitical priesthood," it is saying that priests and Levites serve the Lord together as he has commanded each.

For the rest of the Bible, there will be a distinction between priests and Levites.[10] The sons of Aaron serve at the altar, guard the Most Holy Place, and make sacrifice for the people of Israel (Num. 18:1–3), but the Levites are positioned around the priests and the tabernacle as guardians of both. They are not permitted to enter the inner regions of the tabernacle (Num. 18:4–7), but the Levites do enjoy a blessed place of service nearer to God than the common Israelite.

Ninth, God makes a covenant with the priests and Levites. In Numbers 25 Moses recounts Phinehas's priestly redemption of Levi, which establishes a priestly covenant. In response to an Israelite bringing his sexual sin before Moses and the whole congregation (v. 6), Aaron's grandson picks up his spear and puts the couple to death (vv. 7–8). In their execution, Phinehas removes the plague from camp (vv. 8–9) and atones for the sins of the people (v. 13). Critically, the presence of the plague indicts the Levites, because they should have been doing what Phinehas did. Numbers 8:19 says God gave the Levites to Aaron, "that there may be no plague among the people of Israel when the people of Israel come near the sanctuary." The presence of a "plague" exposes their failure.[11] Yet, as Psalm 106:28–31 indicates, the priestly action of Phinehas is "counted to him as righteousness from generation to generation forever."[12]

---

10. This distinction can even be seen in the parable of the good Samaritan (Luke 10:25–37), where Jesus identifies a priest (v. 31) and then a Levite (v. 32).

11. A similar event of priestly atonement for the sins of Levites occurs in Num. 16:47–50. In this instance, Aaron enters the midst of the people, censer in hand, to make atonement for the plague brought through Korah's rebellion. In both instances, the plague comes because of Levitical disobedience; it ends because of priestly atonement.

12. This verse and Gen. 15:6 are the only two places in the Old Testament where "counted righteous" are used. It is worth remembering that both men who are reckoned righteous are priests—Abraham by his relationship to Melchizedek, Phinehas by his relationship to Aaron.

Incredibly, by leaving his holy precincts and entering the camp, Phinehas purifies the people and restores the Levites to service. Such redemption, which depends on his own righteousness (Ps. 106:31), results in a priestly covenant, as God says in Numbers 25:12–13: "Behold, I give to him my covenant of peace, and it shall be to him and to his descendants after him the covenant of a perpetual priesthood, because he was jealous for his God and made atonement for the people of Israel." The mention of a covenant is critical for understanding the final form of the Levitical priesthood and the foundational "pattern" legislated by Moses. In fact, Malachi most likely has Numbers 25 in mind when he refers to a covenant with Levi, as both passages speak of a "covenant of peace."[13] In this way, Numbers shows us how the arrangement of priests and Levites takes shape.

Tenth, the high priest is established in Israel. In Numbers 35 Moses uses "high priest" for the first time, as he describes the significance of the high priest's death for those who have shed blood (vv. 25, 28 [2x], 32).[14] As Levitical cities are going to be placed in Israel (vv. 1–8), strangers, foreigners, and manslayers are given cities of refuge (vv. 9–15). In cases of unintentional killing, the refuge-seeker is to be protected by Levites *until* the death of the high priest. When the high priest dies, the refugee can leave the refuge city freely. This codicil in the law seems to mean that "the eventual death . . . of the high priest ransomed the death of the victim."[15]

---

13. The Pentateuch makes no mention of a "covenant with Levi"; however, from the terminology employed in Malachi, there is a strong connection between Num. 25:11–13 and Mal. 2:1–9. Douglas Stuart notes nine connections between these passages. Stuart, "Malachi," in *The Minor Prophets: An Exegetical and Expository Commentary*, ed. Thomas E. McComiskey (Grand Rapids, MI: Baker Academic, 1998), 1316–17.

14. As long as Aaron lives, he is the "priest," but when he dies (Num. 20:22–29), the need arises for one of his sons—presumably the eldest—to serve as *high* priest.

15. R. D. Cole, *Numbers*, New American Commentary (Nashville: Broadman & Holman, 2000), 555.

Accordingly, this ransom by the high priest provides the final aspect of Israel's priesthood. As Hebrews will explain, the weakness of the Levitical priesthood is the mortality of its priests (Heb. 7:25–28). It is by this reason of generational death that the order of Aaron can never perfect anyone eternally (Heb. 7:11–14), nor can these priests provide a final ransom. Nevertheless, the office of high priest provides a necessary shadow of the eternal high priest, who will lay down his life once and for all, so that in his resurrection he may be raised to intercede for his people forever.

Eleventh, the priests and Levites are given cities in the land. In the same chapter (Num. 35), Levites are assigned cities throughout Israel. These cities will serve as local outposts of priestly instruction. As T. J. Betts notes, the teaching ministry of the Levitical priesthood (i.e., the priests and Levites) will be carried out throughout the whole land.[16] Or, as we will come to see, it will *fail* to be carried out. This is how the story of the priests and Levites unfolds after the Pentateuch. For now, the distribution of knowledge, which the priests are given (cf. Mal. 2:5–6), is meant to be communicated through these Levitical cities.

Twelfth, the Levitical priesthood is established. After Moses offers thick details concerning priests and Levites in Exodus–Numbers, Deuteronomy has relatively little to say about priests.[17] Nevertheless, Deuteronomy plays an important role in concluding the forty-year story of Israel's priesthood. Most notably, Deuteronomy is the first place where we read the term "Levitical priests" (17:9, 18; 18:1; 24:8; 27:9), as well as "the priests, sons of Levi" (21:5; 31:9).[18]

---

16. T. J. Betts, *Ezekiel the Priest: A Custodian of Tôrâ* (New York: Peter Lang, 2005), 23–24.

17. While Leviticus mentions priests 194 times and Numbers 69 times, Deuteronomy references priests 14 times.

18. It is worth noting that "Levitical priests" could also be rendered "the priests the Levites," as in the KJV and NKJV.

Based on what we have seen so far, the term "Levitical priest" might sound like it unites what should remain separate. Yet in Deuteronomy it is better to see that Moses presents a unified vision of the Levitical priesthood that retains the distinctions established in his previous books. This is most clear in Deuteronomy 18:1–7, where verse 1 begins: "The Levitical priests, all the tribe of Levi, shall have no portion or inheritance with Israel. They shall eat the LORD's food offerings as their inheritance." This verse gives a unified vision for the whole tribe of Levi—whether priests or Levites—and their shared inheritance. Yet the passage goes on to give separate instructions for the priests (vv. 3–5) and the Levites (vv. 6–8). Consistent with Moses's earlier teaching, the priests and Levites remain distinct, even as they work together to serve the Lord.

Importantly, these verses also stress the family structure of Israel's priesthood. As chapters 5–26 expound the Decalogue (5:1–21), Deuteronomy 16:18–18:22 amplifies the fifth commandment: "Honor your father and mother" (5:16).[19] Extending the family structures of Israel to priests and other civic leaders, Moses instructs God's people how to live as a kingdom with priests. Israel should worship God through their brothers in the house of Levi, even as the priests should serve Israel as their own family. This is where the priests will eventually fail, but in Deuteronomy these instructions complete Moses's priestly legislation. And in Deuteronomy 33:8–11 we have one final word concerning the Levitical priesthood:

And of Levi he said,

"Give to Levi your Thummim,
    and your Urim to your godly one,

---

19. Scott Redd, "Deuteronomy," in *A Biblical-Theological Introduction to the Old Testament: The Gospel Promised*, ed. Miles V. Van Pelt (Wheaton, IL: Crossway, 2016), 146–47.

whom you tested at Massah,

> with whom you quarreled at the waters of Meribah;

who said of his father and mother,

> 'I regard them not';

he disowned his brothers

> and ignored his children.

For they observed your word

> and kept your covenant.

They shall teach Jacob your rules

> and Israel your law;

they shall put incense before you

> and whole burnt offerings on your altar.

Bless, O LORD, his substance,

> and accept the work of his hands;

crush the loins of his adversaries,

> of those who hate him, that they rise not again."

These words to the whole house of Levi largely summarize what the Pentateuch has said about the priests and the Levites. In one passage, they encapsulate what the priests do with their brothers, the Levites. Noticeably, by mentioning Massah, Meribah, and the loyalty of the Levites, this passage attends to the priestly storyline we have just followed. It also lists a number of the priestly duties assigned to the Levitical priests (e.g., teaching and offering sacrifices). It is to these priestly duties that we now turn to see the shape of the priesthood that is legislated in the Pentateuch.

The Shape of the Priesthood

If the story of the priesthood requires a broad look across the Pentateuch, the shape of the priesthood can be found in a handful of priestly "job descriptions" (e.g., Lev. 10:11; Deut. 10:8–9; 33:8–11;

cf. 1 Sam. 2:28; 1 Chron. 23:13).[20] These summary lists provide a helpful entry point into what the priests did. That being the case, we can summarize, from the survey we just completed, the actions of the priest under five headings. The priests (1) *stand* to serve in God's house, (2) *guard* God's house and God's people, (3) *offer* sacrifices on God's altar, (4) *teach* God's people, and (5) *intercede* for the people. These five actions are a composite of the priestly duties found in the law, and they support the definition of priesthood offered above, that priests are the *consecrated mediators between God and his covenant people who stand to serve at God's altar, sanctifying God's Holy Place, sacrificing God's offerings, speaking God's covenant.*

The definition synthesizes all of these actions, which are described in multiple places throughout the Pentateuch. In what follows, I will outline what Moses says about these five actions as they give shape to the vocation of the Levitical priests. These summaries will not be long, but they will provide a basic standard by which all the priests in Israel can be evaluated. Thus, by discerning the shape of the priesthood legislated in the Pentateuch, we will be equipped to understand how priests succeed or fail in the rest of the Bible. To that end, let us consider the shape of the Levitical priesthood.

First, priests stand to serve in God's presence. Exodus 28 is the place where Aaron and his sons are chosen by God to "draw near" to the Lord. Verse 1 says, "Then bring near to you Aaron your brother, and his sons with him, from among the people of Israel, to serve me as priests—Aaron and Aaron's sons, Nadab and Abihu, Eleazar and Ithamar." The verb "draw near" is often associated with priests, worship, and sacrifice. In Leviticus 1–7 it is used forty-eight times to describe the act of bringing a sacrifice to the altar. Likewise, Moses

---

20. Richard D. Nelson, *Raising Up a Faithful Priest: Community and Priesthood in Biblical Theology* (Louisville: Westminster John Knox, 1993), 39.

says to Aaron in Leviticus 9:7, "Draw near to the altar and offer your sin offering and your burnt offering and make atonement for yourself and for the people, and bring the offering of the people and make atonement for them, as the LORD has commanded." This service at the altar is the chief work of the priests. It is what sets them apart from the Levites and the rest of Israel. After Exodus 28, only Aaron and his sons are permitted by God to stand at the altar.

In time, serving in God's house and standing at his altar will become shorthand for priestly service. While land is withheld from Aaron and his sons, their superior inheritance is found in their proximity to God. Yahweh says to Aaron in Numbers 18:20: "You shall have no inheritance in their land, neither shall you have any portion among them. I am your portion and your inheritance among the people of Israel."[21] In short, the Levitical priesthood is consecrated to focus singularly on serving the Lord at his house. It is appropriate, therefore, to see priests as "attendants in Yahweh's house," always ready to do his bidding.[22] The four following actions (guarding, sacrificing, teaching, and interceding) are then the services they will render in that sacred place, mediating the relationship between God and his covenant people.

Second, priests guard God's house. As guardians of Yahweh's house, the priests are called to make sure that nothing unclean approaches the Lord and his holiness. In Numbers 3, the priests are stationed before the gate of the tabernacle courtyard. As verse 38 indicates: "Those who were to camp before the tabernacle on the east, before the tent of meeting toward the sunrise, were Moses and Aaron and his sons, guarding the sanctuary itself, to protect the people of Israel.

---

21. The importance of this priestly inheritance resurfaces throughout Israel's history: Deut. 10:9; 12:12; 14:27; 18:1–2; Josh. 13:14, 33; 14:3; 18:7; Ezek. 44:28.

22. Peter J. Leithart, "Attendants of Yahweh's House: Priesthood in the Old Testament," *Journal for the Study of the Old Testament* 24, no. 85 (1999).

And any outsider who came near was to be put to death." In a chapter detailing the service of the Levites, this instruction for the priests is the final word.

With the Levites, the priests stand between the people and God. They protect the people from God's anger toward their sin, and they protect God's house from the uncleanness of the people. In Numbers 3, the Levites guard the perimeter of the courtyard, and they guard their brothers, the priests, too (vv. 5–8). The priests guard the precincts closer to the altar, especially the holy furniture within the tabernacle itself. Together, the priests and Levites maintain the holiness of God's dwelling place.

Third, priests offer sacrifices on the altar. Though the Levites assist their brothers in guarding God's dwelling place, the law does not permit them to bring sacrifices to the altar. This is the role uniquely assigned to Aaron and his sons. Exodus 28–29 explains what it takes to consecrate the priests for service—a series of sacrifices and washings for purification. Likewise, Leviticus 8–9 explains the process of purifying Aaron and his sons so that they may approach the altar. Only after being purified with blood and water may Aaron "draw near to the altar" (9:8). Then, the first thing he must do is offer a sacrifice to cover his own sins (9:8). Only after making atonement for himself can he turn and bless the people (9:8–22). The presence of God's glory depends on a holy priest offering an acceptable sacrifice on a pure altar. Indeed, the importance of their sacrificial ministry is seen in the way everything else in Israel's worship depends upon the priests.

In Leviticus, the first seven chapters detail the five types of sacrifice. Leviticus 16 explains the annual sacrifice that the high priest brings into the Most Holy Place. And Leviticus 23 organizes the calendar around the festivals of Israel, with each including the offering of sacrifices. In short, every form of worship in the Old Testament centers on the priests and their sacrificial duties. To borrow the language of Hebrews 9:22, without the shedding of blood there is no remission of sins. And it is from the altar itself that priests pronounce forgiveness for God's people (see, e.g., Lev. 4:20, 26, 31, 35; 5:10, 13). Without the priests applying blood to the altar, there can be no forgiveness or fellowship with God. As Deuteronomy 33:10 says of the priests, "They shall put incense before you and whole burnt offerings on your altar." In all these ways, we see why the sacrificial ministry of the priests is so central.[23]

Fourth, priests teach the covenant to God's people. The priests focus their ministry on the sacrifices they bring to the Lord, but they also commence an important ministry of teaching. After Nadab and Abihu die because of their unauthorized approach to God's altar, we read, "You are to distinguish between the holy and the common, and between the unclean and the clean, and you are to teach the people of Israel all the statutes that the LORD has spoken to them by Moses" (Lev. 10:10–11). This is a key passage for understanding the teaching ministry of the priests. The priests' teaching role is often underappreciated, but it will become one of the most important aspects of their service. The call to distinguish clean from unclean, as in cases of leprosy (Lev. 13–14), is one way priests minister God's word and make sure God's people have a knowledge of the covenant (cf. Mal. 2:1–9).

Truly, the sons of Aaron are keepers of the covenant, making them responsible for ensuring that Israel walks with God (cf. Lev. 23–27). Moreover, the priests, as conduits of God's mercy, have been called to speak God's blessing upon the people of Israel. This is what Numbers

---

23. To be clear, the blood of bulls and goats could never *ultimately* atone for sin, but the work of the Levitical priest served its purpose in time—to cleanse the flesh and permit Israel to dwell in the presence of God.

6:24–26 records in the words of the Aaronic blessing. When God's people walk with the Lord, it is because the priests call the people to know the Lord and pronounce God's blessing upon them.

As with the work of guarding Yahweh's house, the priests share this role of teaching with their brothers, the Levites. Put differently, the priests teach the nation through the ministry of the Levites. Moreover, Deuteronomy 17:18–20 commissions the Levitical priests to watch over the king as he transcribes the law; Deuteronomy 31:9–13 calls for the priests to read the law publicly every seven years; and Deuteronomy 33:10 states most plainly, "They shall teach Jacob your rules and Israel your law." For these reasons, the priests not only have the responsibility to atone for the sins of Israel but also have the duty to call Israel to keep covenant with God. This is why Malachi would say of the priests, "For the lips of a priest should guard knowledge, and people should seek instruction from his mouth, for he is the messenger of the LORD of hosts" (Mal. 2:7).

Fifth and finally, priests intercede for the people. Standing between God and man, the priests intercede for the well-being of God's people. This service of prayer is modeled by Moses in Exodus 32–34, when Israel sins against God. It is also displayed by Aaron after the plague afflicts Israel because of Korah's rebellion. In Numbers 16:46–48, Moses says to Aaron:

> "Take your censer, and put fire on it from off the altar and lay incense on it and carry it quickly to the congregation and make atonement for them, for wrath has gone out from the LORD; the plague has begun." So Aaron took it as Moses said and ran into the midst of the assembly. And behold, the plague had already begun among the people. And he put on the incense and made atonement for the people. And

he stood between the dead and the living, and the plague
was stopped.

In this incident Aaron goes among the people with the incense of
the altar to atone for the people through his intercession. God shows
mercy on Israel as Aaron intercedes. This proactive response to Israel's sin shows the kind of role priests are to have in Israel, and it
demonstrates how atonement and intercession are inseparable.

More typically, priests offer incense in the tabernacle itself (Ex.
30:22–38). Clothed in garments that bear the names of Israel (Ex.
28:1–43), the priests thereby bring to remembrance the people of
Israel before God (vv. 12, 29). Later, in Psalm 141:2, prayer will be
associated with the altar of incense. Likewise, Aaron is said to call
upon the name of the Lord (Ps. 99:6), which is a way of describing
prayer (see Gen. 4:26). From these passages, we can reasonably infer
that the priest's ministry of intercession includes prayer and bringing
the people of God before the Lord at the altar of incense.

The Shadow of the Priesthood Points to Christ

What God gives us in the law of Moses is the idealized pattern of
priesthood in Israel. It is debatable whether any priest ever lived
up to all these standards. In this way, these priestly duties, which
developed over the course of Moses's forty-year ministry, serve as
a shadow of the true priesthood to come. Just as the tabernacle is a
pattern of the heavenly tabernacle that will eventually come to earth
in the ministry of Jesus Christ (Ex. 25:9, 40), so the priesthood is a
shadow that will find its true substance in the great priesthood of
Jesus Christ.

Indeed, in the Pentateuch itself we become aware of the weakness
of Aaron's priesthood. While Aaron and his sons will be strengthened
and supported by the Levites, there remains an intrinsic weakness in

their priesthood. Sin and death will continue to darken the light that the priests bring to the people. And thus, even as we should rejoice in the ministry of the priesthood given to Israel, we can see why it is no longer in service. It was given for a time and for the purpose of being replaced by a better priesthood. That priesthood has come in Christ. Yet, to appreciate Christ's priesthood, we need to see how the Levitical system succeeded and failed as Israel entered the land. To that next step in the journey, we now turn.

3

The Prophets

The Priesthood Promised, Compromised, and Promised Again

A few years ago, our family moved into a new home. With an army of glad-hearted servants, we painted walls, cleaned floors, and assembled furniture. In that first month, our home looked grand. But quickly our sons did what busy boys do—they spilled drinks, threw balls, and turned walls into their own canvas space. In a remarkably short time, the glory of our home faded, requiring constant upkeep and repair.

When Israel crossed the Jordan, something similar occurred, and the glory of the tabernacle needed constant attention as well. This attention to God's house, which we learned of in the last chapter, was assigned to the Levitical priests. Standing before Yahweh, the sons of Aaron lived to sanctify God's house and God's people. Assisted by a family system of priests and Levites, the high priest brought Israel before the Lord by offering incense on the golden altar. In the other direction, the high priest brought God's presence to Israel as he pronounced God's blessing upon them. Through this multidirectional service, the Levitical priesthood helped Israel keep covenant, so that the nation might enjoy God's blessing. In fact, it is not too much to say that the status of the nation depended upon the faithfulness of the priests and Levites.

Looking at this relationship between priest and people, we can divide it into three historical stages. The first stage is found in Joshua and displays what happens when Levitical priests fulfill their ministry. The second stage begins in Judges and continues to the end of the Old Testament, as priests begin to compromise their duties. Last, in the third stage, which overlaps with the second stage, the Prophets begin to promise a new priesthood that will replace the Levitical priesthood. Put together, the storyline of Israel's priesthood looks something like a check mark (✓). The priesthood begins at the top in Joshua, it drops throughout the history of Israel, and it promises to rise again, to even greater heights, in Israel's future. In this chapter, we will consider each of these stages.

The Promise of the Levitical Priesthood

Of all the books in the Old Testament, Joshua is the one where the priests are most faithful. How do we know? First, nothing in Joshua indicts them for breaking God's commands. Second, everywhere the priests are found, they are faithfully assisting Joshua and effectively serving the nation. Third, the priests' service leads to God's people enjoying God's blessings.

Indeed, from standing in the Jordan River holding the ark of the covenant (Josh. 3), to assisting in Yahweh's defeat of Jericho (Josh. 6), to their forthcoming placement in the land (Josh. 21), to Phinehas's peacemaking (Josh. 22), the Levitical priests are nothing but a blessing in Joshua. As we saw chapter 2, this is why God put the priests in place, so they could mediate blessing. In Joshua the priests are off to a promising start, and such faithfulness provides a baseline for all future generations. Two traits mark this time.

First, the priests enable God's people to draw near to God. In Deuteronomy 12, Yahweh tells Israel that he will put his name in the land, at a place of his choosing.[1] This means that entrance into the land will bring God's people nearer to the place where Yahweh will dwell during the days of Israel. Some have even considered Israel's entrance into Canaan a "return to Eden," as God's people reentered the place where God will meet them.[2] Importantly, drawing near to God in the land comes through Joshua and the service of the priests.

Beginning in Joshua 3–4, we find an army of priests carrying the ark across the Jordan, their feet turning back the water and making a way for Israel to walk on dry ground. These same priests carry the ark around Jericho (Josh. 6:12), as seven priests blow seven trumpets to knock down Jericho's walls (Josh. 6:4, 6, 8–9, 13, 15–21). When Joshua leads Israel to renew their covenant (8:30–35), the priests stand in service around the ark (v. 33). As the people of Israel receive their various places in Canaan, Eleazar "the priest" helps distribute the inheritance (see Josh. 14:1; 17:4; 19:51; 21:2). Even more, as Joshua sets up the tabernacle in Shiloh (19:51; 21:2), the Levites receive "cities and pasturelands" amid the twelve tribes (21:1–42). In all, the service of the priests enables Israel to draw near to God and dwell with him in the land. Without the Levitical priests, communion with God—defined as it was by the covenant at Sinai—would not have been possible.

---

1. In Joshua, this place is Shiloh (see Josh. 18:1–10). Later, David will establish God's place in Jerusalem, where the temple of the Lord is built by Solomon.

2. If the Promised Land is a new Eden, it only heightens the connection between Adam and Israel, and the priestly identity of each.

Second, the Levitical priests facilitate worship for God's people. As we have observed previously, sanctifying God's Holy Place, speaking God's words (i.e., instructing God's people and interceding for them), and offering sacrifices on the altar are the three main actions of a priest. And in Joshua, during a period of remarkable obedience, we see all three.

For instance, the Levitical priests carry the ark of the covenant and make sure the people maintain a proper distance (3:3–4). Likewise, in setting up the tabernacle in Shiloh, the whole nation is oriented around this central place of worship (Josh. 13–19).[3] Then, when the people are finally settled in the land and the Eastern tribes build an altar of witness, it is Phinehas "the priest" (22:30–32) who goes and checks on its purpose. Indeed, throughout Joshua the priests are proactive in maintaining the purity of God's tabernacle and seeking the purity of God's people.

The priests also assist Joshua in renewing the covenant and proclaiming God's word. While Joshua takes the lead in chapter 8, the priests are present and active, witnessing to the blessings and the curses of the covenant found in Deuteronomy 27–28.[4] This priestly ministry of proclamation will continue as the Levites are placed in the land (Josh. 21). In fact, Joshua continues to stress that the inheritance of the priests and the Levites is not land but God himself (13:14, 33; 14:3–4; 18:7). This highlights their appointment to serve God and his people.

Last, Joshua 5:10–12 records the first Passover in the land. In this episode, the nation as a whole remembers the event that set them apart and made them a kingdom of priests. Similarly, Joshua 18:1–10

---

3. Joshua 13–21 demonstrates a literary structure that places the sanctuary and the sons of Levi in the center (18:1–10) of all the other tribes.

4. At this point, it is worth mentioning that there are good reasons for seeing Joshua as acting as a priestly leader, like Moses. The scope of this book, however, does not permit an inquiry into the priestly actions of Joshua.

records the establishment of the tabernacle at Shiloh. While nothing is said about sacrifices, the obedience of Joshua and the priests suggests that the sacrifices required by Moses are now in place, and that Eleazar "the priest" has begun to serve Israel as a high priest.

From another angle, we might observe how the sacrifices offered in Joshua are the cities devoted to destruction. Deuteronomy 20:1–9 says that the priests prepare the army for battle, and Numbers 10:8–9 and 31:6 call the priests to blow the silver trumpets to lead the nation into war. Putting this into practice, the Levitical priests join Joshua on the battlefield to make sure the warfare is holy and acceptable to God. In this stage of Israel's history, the priests are active in purifying the place where God's people will live, so that when the land has rest (Josh. 14:1), they can stand before God and minister at his altar.

In the end, we can see in Joshua how faithful priests bless God's people. That being the case, their positive impact on Israel will be short-lived. Joshua 24:29 reports Joshua's death, and Joshua 24:33 reports the death of Eleazar "the son of Aaron." With these deaths, Israel enters a new phase of history. And while priests will continue to play a central role, they will never live up to the promise of the priests who have served alongside Joshua.

The Compromise of the Levitical Priesthood

Warning signs for the priesthood begin as soon as Joshua and his generation die. In Judges, we find these sad words: "And all that generation also were gathered to their fathers. And there arose another generation after them who did not know the LORD or the work that he had done for Israel" (2:10). Though nothing is said about priests, this verse raises the question How could the next generation not know the Lord, unless the priests failed to teach them? In Judges, this question is answered by the conspicuous absence of the Levitical priests. Instead of leading the people into the presence of God and interceding on their behalf, as they did in Joshua, the priests fail to make their mark.

In the first sixteen chapters of Judges, no priest is mentioned. And when the word "priest" shows up in chapters 17–19, it describes a pair of Levites who exalt themselves as faux priests—an action reminiscent of Korah (cf. Num. 16). Adding to this story of compromise, 1 Samuel reveals what the absent priests are doing. They are serving themselves at the tabernacle—violating women and exploiting the people. In short, what God intended the priests to be, and what they were under Joshua, is no more. For the rest of the Old Testament, with occasional counterexamples and seasons of revival, compromise will continue.

Though we cannot look at every historical detail, we should familiarize ourselves with the elements of priestly compromise. For in seeing how the priests deviate from God's design, we will see why the Levitical priesthood will fail and why a new priesthood will be needed. In particular, we find four ways the priests compromise their priestly position and fail to keep their priestly duties.

Failure to Obey the Law

Failure to obey God's law is immediately apparent in Judges 17. First, a man named Micah hires a Levite to replace his own son as a priest (vv. 1–13). Rather than reproving Micah for building his own altar, this Levite abandons the law and the Lord at Shiloh (Judg. 18:31). "Instead of serving as an agent of life and peace, revering Yahweh and standing in awe of his name, offering truthful and righteous instruction, walking with knowledge, and serving as a messenger of Yahweh of hosts, this Levite has himself apostasized."[5]

---

5. Daniel I. Block, *Judges, Ruth*, New American Commentary (Nashville: Broadman & Holman, 1999), 490.

Tragically, the waywardness of the Levitical priesthood continues in Judges 18–19. While priests retain their position to teach (cf. Lev. 10:11), Judges demonstrates the brokenness of the system and the need for a king who will reestablish the priesthood. In Joshua, God's chosen ruler led Israel with faithful priests, but in Judges, the people do what is right in their own eyes, and there is no king in Israel (17:6; 21:25). This closing refrain shows that Israel has abandoned God as their king and that the Levitical priests are not calling them back to the Lord. Still, in Judges all that can be said is that they are delinquent in their duties. It is not until 1 Samuel, which begins in the days of the judges, that we discover why.

In 1 Samuel 1–4 we meet the priest Eli and his wicked sons, Hophni and Phinehas.[6] First Samuel 2 says that these sons "did not know the LORD" (v. 12). They "treated the offering of the LORD with contempt" (v. 17), abused the people they served (vv. 15–16), committed sexual immorality with "the women who were serving at the entrance to the tent of meeting" (v. 22), and disobeyed their father when he confronted them in their sin (vv. 22–25).[7] As a result, "the word of the LORD was rare" in those days (3:2). Because teaching is a priestly vocation, this dearth of covenantal knowledge demonstrates Eli's failure. That Samuel could grow up in the house of the Lord and "not yet know the LORD" is equally shocking (3:7). It confirms the lawless condition during the time of the judges, and it sets up how God is about to reverse the situation. In 1 Samuel 2, God announces the end of Eli's priesthood (vv. 27–34) and the arrival of a "faithful priest" (v. 35).

---

6. This is not the same Phinehas we find in Numbers and Joshua.

7. The Bible also suggests that Eli was unfit to serve as Israel's priest. Evidence of Eli's unfaithfulness: He confused Hannah's prayer with drunkenness (1 Sam. 1:14) and failed to recognize God's voice to Samuel (1 Sam. 3:4–9). He passively ignored the sins of his sons, and God's judgment came upon him for this reason: "On that day I will fulfill against Eli all that I have spoken concerning his house, from beginning to end. And I declare to him that I am about to punish his house forever, for the iniquity that he knew, because his sons were blaspheming God, and he did not restrain them" (1 Sam. 3:12–13).

The rest of 1–2 Samuel records a history of Israel's first two kings, Saul and David, and their contrasting relationships to God, his word, and the priesthood. In fact, throughout the rest of the Old Testament there will be a close and conflicted relationship between the kings of Israel and the priests who serve at God's house. For now, we should acknowledge that before David replaces Saul as Israel's true king, the Levitical priesthood already stumbles. In Judges we find two Levites asserting themselves to be priests. Likewise, in the opening chapters of 1 Samuel, Eli, Hophni, and Phinehas all die because of their disobedience before God. Such is the danger of being an imposter or a disobedient priest. When men exalt themselves to be priests and when true priests fail to keep God's covenant, they endanger God's people and invite their own downfall.

Such is the basic premise of priestly service—to stand as a servant in God's house requires unrelenting commitment to God and his word. Otherwise, the glory of God will depart, as when the Philistines take the ark of the covenant from the sons of Eli (1 Sam. 4:21–22). In addition to neglecting their teaching duties, the priests at Shiloh fail to guard the tabernacle and its most important piece of furniture—the ark. Now, without the mercy seat of God, which sits on the top of the ark of the covenant, the priests cannot atone for people's sin, nor can they continue to serve as priests. This is not the way it was meant to be. Yet, sadly, this will be an ongoing pattern for priests in Israel. Priests will fail to guard God's holiness, instruct God's people, and offer holy sacrifices—the three actions that define the priesthood.

Failure to Guard God's Holy Dwelling

Before and after God grants kingship to the house of David (2 Sam. 7), the Levitical priests struggle to maintain the purity of God's house. This is evident in the opening chapters of 1 Samuel, and it is also true during the reign of Judean kings like Ahaz (2 Kings 16) and Manasseh (2 Kings 21). Among the Northern tribes of Israel, Jeroboam fabricates an entire system of worship to rival the temple in Jerusalem (1 Kings 12–13). This false worship consists of making worship centers in Dan and Bethel (12:26–29), fashioning two golden calves (12:28), replacing the Day of Atonement with a different festival (12:31–33), and installing his own priests instead of priests and Levites (2 Chron. 11:14–15). In short, the history of Israel demonstrates that the kings influence the priests and the priests fail to instruct the kings, as Deuteronomy 17:18–20 required. As a result, the Latter Prophets regularly condemn the priests for their failure to guard their holiness and God's holy temple.

For example, Ezekiel watches the Spirit abandon God's temple because the priests have failed to guard it from idolatry (Ezek. 8–11). We learn from Ezekiel 8:1–18 that Israel's elders are permitted to worship idols in the temple, and later we find that the priests do not stop Gentiles from approaching God's altar (44:5–8). Because God can no longer abide with such sin in his dwelling place, his glory departs.[8] Just as God's glory left the tabernacle at Shiloh, now God's glory departs from Jerusalem (cf. Jer. 7:8–15).

Ezekiel is not alone in his priestly indictment. Before and after Ezekiel, we find prophets addressing priestly compromise. Hosea, for instance, compares the priests to a band of robbers (6:9). Micah says that the priests "teach for a price" (3:11). Zephaniah promises that the idolatrous priests will be cut off (1:4–6). And Zechariah sees a vision of Joshua the high priest in "filthy garments," symbolizing his iniquity (Zech. 3:4–5). All of these iniquities reveal why the priests cannot keep God's house pure. Motivated by avarice and indifferent

---

8. Notice the reenactment of 1 Sam. 1–4 in Ezek. 8–11: the priests of Israel display egregious wickedness in God's house, and the result is "Ichabod"—the glory has departed (1 Sam. 4:21–22).

toward idolatry, generations of priests defile themselves and God's house. Ultimately, this is why the Lord declares in Malachi 2:1–3:

> And now, O priests, this command is for you. If you will not listen, if you will not take it to heart to give honor to my name, says the LORD of hosts, then I will send the curse upon you and I will curse your blessings. Indeed, I have already cursed them, because you do not lay it to heart. Behold, I will rebuke your offspring, and spread dung on your faces, the dung of your offerings, and you shall be taken away with it.

In Israel's history, there are exceptions to this downward trend of the priests, but these are very few.[9] Levitical priests repeatedly fail to guard the holiness of their office and God's house.

FAILURE TO INSTRUCT THE PEOPLE

The Levitical priests also fail to instruct God's people. While things begin well when David and Solomon establish the temple, they soon unravel. Addressing the Northern tribes, Hosea 4:6 declares:

> My people are destroyed for lack of knowledge;
>> because you have rejected knowledge,
>> I reject you from being a priest to me.
> And since you have forgotten the law of your God,
>> I also will forget your children.

Though the whole nation suffers for their sin, the Lord lays particular blame on his priests. In Jeremiah, the same problem occurs. Jeremiah 2:8 declares,

---

9. For instance, Jehoiada the priest leads a revolt against the wicked queen Athaliah and preserves the royal line of David (2 Kings 11–12). Likewise, Azariah the chief priest leads a band of priests to remove Uzziah from the temple when the king of Judah offers incense on the altar (2 Chron. 26:16–23).

The priests did not say, "Where is the LORD?"

Those who handle the law did not know me;

the shepherds transgressed against me;

the prophets prophesied by Baal

and went after things that do not profit.

(cf. 6:10, 13–14; 14:18)

Much as in the days of the judges, the nation is ignorant because the priests have not taught the law. They have served themselves and turned their holy calling into a "moneymaking racket."[10] As a result, God disowns the priests because they do not keep covenant with him. As Malachi 2:6–9 says of the priests:

> True instruction was in his mouth, and no wrong was found on his lips. He walked with me in peace and uprightness, and he turned many from iniquity. For the lips of a priest should guard knowledge, and people should seek instruction from his mouth, for he is the messenger of the LORD of hosts. But you have turned aside from the way. You have caused many to stumble by your instruction. You have corrupted the covenant of Levi, says the LORD of hosts, and so I make you despised and abased before all the people, inasmuch as you do not keep my ways but show partiality in your instruction.

FAILURE TO OFFER HOLY SACRIFICES ON GOD'S ALTAR

If the priests fail to guard God's house and instruct the people, it's not surprising that they also offer impure sacrifices. Evidence of impure and absent sacrifices is found in multiple places. First, the presence of two worship centers in Dan and Bethel indicates that a whole segment of Israel is pursuing idolatrous worship on false altars. Though

---

10. Leslie C. Allen, *Joel, Obadiah, Jonah, and Micah*, New International Commentary on the Old Testament (Grand Rapids, MI: Eerdmans, 1976), 318.

the Levitical priests continue to serve in Jerusalem, prophets like Hosea and Amos take aim to rebuke the sacrifices offered outside Jerusalem. Hosea 8:11, for instance, states, "Because Ephraim has multiplied altars for sinning, they have become to him altars for sinning." And taking aim at Jerusalem, Amos 5:21–22 reads:

> I hate, I despise your feasts,
>> and I take no delight in your solemn assemblies.
> Even though you offer me your burnt offerings and grain
>> offerings,
>> I will not accept them;
> and the peace offerings of your fattened animals,
>> I will not look upon them.

These indictments are reinforced by Joel, who calls for priests to stand and intercede between the temple building and the altar in the courtyard (2:17). He cannot call the priests to offer sacrifices, because famine and locusts have annihilated the crops needed to bring oil and bread to the temple (1:2–13). Thus, he recalls the words of Exodus 34:6 ("a God merciful and gracious, slow to anger, and abounding in steadfast love") and summons the priests to seek God's mercy (Joel 2:13). Such a need reveals that the regular worship of God in the tabernacle has ceased (Joel 1:13), and this unwelcome hiatus is due to Israel's covenant unfaithfulness. As we saw above, priestly negligence in guarding holiness and teaching the people contributes to the curses of God, and now Joel is calling the priests to seek God's mercy, that they may again offer right sacrifices.

In all, there are many periods in Israel's history when Israel offers worthless sacrifices. Hosea 6:6 records the word of Yahweh: "I desire steadfast love and not sacrifice." God's anger at false sacrifices does not overturn the need for sacrifice; his anger concerns sacrifices offered without faith. At the same time, improper sacrifices offered by uncaring priests are equally odious. Whereas God intends the sacrifices to be a pleasing aroma before him, unclean and blemished sacrifices only invite wrath. As Malachi 1:7 observes, the priests offer polluted food on God's altar. Instead of treating God with proper holiness, they treat him with contempt. Malachi 1:13–14 records Yahweh's words to the priests:

> You bring what has been taken by violence or is lame or sick, and this you bring as your offering! Shall I accept that from your hand? says the LORD. Cursed be the cheat who has a male in his flock, and vows it, and yet sacrifices to the Lord what is blemished. For I am a great King, says the LORD of hosts, and my name will be feared among the nations.

This final statement promises that a day is coming when God's name will be feared—not only in Israel but in all the nations. As Malachi 1:11 states: "For from the rising of the sun to its setting my name will be great among the nations, and in every place incense will be offered to my name, and a pure offering. For my name will be great among the nations, says the LORD of hosts." This promise of a pure offering, which is set in the midst of God's condemnation of the priests, reminds us of the central place that priests and their sacrifices play in God's plan of salvation.

The only problem is that in Israel, the priests fail to live up to their high calling. Instead, from generation to generation, they compromise their obedience by failing to guard God's holiness, instruct God's people, and offer pure sacrifices. For these reasons, the prophets condemn the priests. Yet the prophets also promise that a greater priest will come. In Malachi, the unswerving condemnation of the priests is not the final word. Instead, the last two chapters of Malachi promise a restoration of the priesthood and the kingdom. Only, as we will see, this promise of a greater priesthood is not a return to the Levitical system. Rather, as all the prophets indicate, a new covenant is coming, and with it will come a true and better royal priesthood.

The Better Promise of a Royal Priesthood

Perhaps it is surprising that the first promise of a new priest does not come at the end of the Old Testament. Instead, it is mentioned in 1 Samuel, in the days when the sons of Eli are rebelling against God. As we saw previously, Hophni and Phinehas invite the wrath of God by their wicked rebellion. In their day, they are handed over to death and their priesthood is taken from them (2:30–35).[11] In this context of judgment, we find the promise of a new priesthood. Proclaimed by an unknown prophet (2:27), verse 35 reads: "I will raise up for myself a faithful priest, who shall do according to what is in my heart and in my mind. And I will build him a sure house, and he shall go in and out before my anointed forever."

Like so many promises in the Bible, this one is pregnant with meaning, and it will take the rest of the Bible to develop. As Israel's history unfolds, various prophets will add to the picture of this "faithful priest," until a full-fledged vision of a new and better priest emerges. Significantly, we will see that these prophetic additions result in the hope of a *royal* priest, not a *Levitical* priest. Or to put it differently, there begins to arise a hope of a righteous king who will offer a sacrifice that brings about a new covenant that secures forgiveness for sins forever!

As we will see in the remainder of this chapter, the rise of a royal priest, or a king with priestly devotion, is something that begins

---

11. First Kings 2:27 reports the fulfillment of this judgment: Solomon "expelled Abiathar from being priest to the LORD, thus fulfilling the word of the LORD that he had spoken concerning the house of Eli in Shiloh."

in the life of David. In the Latter Prophets, the promise of a royal priest becomes explicit, as multiple prophets voice that promise. At the same time, as these prophets speak, there is the renewed hope that this royal priest will establish a new kingdom of priests, comprising God's redeemed people—both Jews and Gentiles. Truly, this is the high point of the check mark. Whereas the Levitical priests under Joshua offered a vision of what the law could do, the prophets foretell of a priesthood that far exceeds anything Israel ever experienced. Indeed, what we will see in the prophets is what Christ alone can accomplish when he comes as a priest after the order of Melchizedek.[12]

KINGS WITH PRIESTLY DEVOTION

To see how this promise of a royal priest develops, we begin with the way kings and priests interact in Israel. In particular, we should see how David is presented as a *priestly* kind of king. While not calling him a priest, 1–2 Samuel presents David in many priestly ways.

To begin with, the language of a "sure house" in 1 Samuel 2:35 is remarkably similar to God's promise of a "sure house" in 2 Samuel 7, the place where God promises David an eternal throne. In 1 Samuel 2, God promises this new priest that he "will build him a sure house." In 2 Samuel 7, God promises to make David a house (v. 11) and adds: "Your house and your kingdom shall be made sure forever before me. Your throne shall be established forever" (v. 16). By comparing these statements, we find two complementary promises—God will build a "sure" priestly house and a "sure" royal house.[13] And what is

---

12. A "priest forever after the order of Melchizedek" is terminology that comes in the Writings (Ps. 110:4). It is appropriate (and necessary) to read the prophetic vision of a royal priest in light of Ps. 110, and vice versa.

13. The word in both instances is the same. And importantly, David himself is recognized as being the most "faithful" servant in Saul's kingdom (1 Sam. 22:14).

noteworthy is the way 1 and 2 Samuel intersect and overlap these promises in David's life.

For instance, David brings the ark to Jerusalem (2 Sam. 6:12–15; cf. Josh. 3:3; 8:33), offers sacrifices (2 Sam. 6:17), and blesses the people (2 Sam. 6:19).[14] This combination alerts us to the ways in which David is acting like a priest. Furthering his priestly role, 2 Samuel 6:14 describes David wearing a priestly ephod. In this scene, the author overlaps David's royal office with his priestly attire as this faithful king brings the ark into the city of God Most High. While Melchizedek is not named in this episode, it is hard not to think of this royal priestly figure, especially when David purchases the threshing floor of Araunah to build an altar and offer a sacrifice to atone for his sin (2 Sam. 24:18–25). In buying this location, David acquires the place where Abraham offered the ram for Isaac and where Solomon would build the temple (see 2 Chron. 3:1). In all these ways, the reader is left to wonder what is going on between David's kingship and his preoccupation with the priesthood.[15]

Recognizing that the combination of priest and king is not formalized in the days of David, we can begin to see why David could say of his son Solomon—or Jesus, depending on how one reads Psalm 110—that he is a priest forever after the order of Melchizedek (v. 4). Indeed, if in David's own lifetime he does many priestly things and his sons are called "priests" (2 Sam. 8:18), how much more will

---

14. Carl E. Armerding, "Were David's Sons Really Priests?," in *Current Issues in Biblical and Patristic Interpretation*, ed. Gerald F. Hawthorne (Grand Rapids, MI: Eerdmans, 1975), 75–86; cf. Eugene H. Merrill, "Royal Priesthood: An Old Testament Messianic Motif," *Bibliotheca Sacra* 150 (1993): 50–61.

15. Another evidence supporting David's priestly commitments can be found in a comparison between Saul and David. As a king like those of the nations, who takes from the people of God (see 1 Sam. 8:10–18), Saul will exploit and even execute the priests of Israel (1 Sam. 22). By contrast, David, as a righteous king, will protect the priests in Israel. He will look to establish God's dwelling place in Jerusalem and, as 1 Chron. 22–26 explains, will set up the priests and the Levites in Jerusalem too. This does not make David a priest, but it does distinguish his kingship as one that protects and patronizes the Levitical priesthood.

his Son Jesus Christ be recognized as a royal priest. In truth, this fusion of priest and king is not yet clear in the days of David, but as we turn to the Latter Prophets, what is hidden in the original promise of 1 Samuel 2:35 becomes more visible.

THE PROMISE OF A ROYAL PRIEST

Two of the clearest statements about a coming royal priest are found in Jeremiah and Zechariah. First, Jeremiah 30:21 states,

> Their prince shall be one of themselves;
>> their ruler shall come out from their midst;
> I will make him draw near, and he shall approach me,
>> for who would dare of himself to approach me?
>>>> declares the LORD.

The invitation to "draw near" clarifies that this action is priestly (cf. Ex. 28:1), and the use of the word "prince" identifies this man as a son of David (cf. 2 Sam. 7:8). In the context of Jeremiah 30–33, the new covenant will come by means of this prince's priestly service.

Likewise, the blessings of the new covenant indicate that, unlike the Sinai covenant, which resulted in a separation between people and priests, this new covenant will be one where all of the covenant members are priests to one another. As we observed in the law, the people approach God through a complex of priests and Levites. With the new covenant, however, everyone will know the Lord (Jer. 31:34), and they will not need other human mediators. Instead, all members of the new covenant will know God and participate in the priestly ministry of this covenant. We will consider the priesthood of believers more fully when we get to the New Testament.

Second, Zechariah gives us an explicit vision of royal priesthood. In Zechariah 3:1–10, the prophet sees Joshua the high priest purified on earth, which reflects the greater purity of God's priest in heaven. Likewise, Zechariah 6:12–14 says:

> Thus says the LORD of hosts, "Behold, the man whose name is the Branch: for he shall branch out from his place, and he shall build the temple of the LORD. It is he who shall build the temple of the LORD and shall bear royal honor and shall sit and rule on his throne. And there shall be a priest on his throne, and the counsel of peace shall be between them both." And the crown shall be in the temple of the LORD.

These two passages, plus Zechariah 9–14, tell of a day when "cleansing from sin and uncleanness" will come to the house of David (13:1) and then from David's house to the world (Zech. 12–14). Indeed, while Zechariah 6 promises to join priest and king together, Zechariah 3 explains how this will happen.[16]

In one of his night visions, Zechariah records the angel of the Lord shutting the mouth of Satan, the accuser (vv. 1–2), ordering purification for Joshua the high priest (vv. 3–5), restoring the covenant with Levi (vv. 6–7), and raising the Levitical priesthood as a "sign" foreshadowing a greater priest. More specifically, Joshua's priestly associates ("friends") are the sign that divine growth (i.e., "the Branch") is coming (v. 8).[17] The priestly nature of this growth is seen in the holy garments, turban, and etched headstone, as well as the reference to the Day of Atonement, when sin will be removed from the land in a single day (v. 9). "In that day" the kingdom, symbolized by a vine

---

16. Space does not permit a discussion of Zech. 9–14, which anticipates the coming of God's royal shepherd to Jerusalem (9:9–13) and his subsequent sacrifice, which establishes a new covenant (13:7–11).

17. Peter J. Gentry and Stephen J. Wellum, *Kingdom through Covenant: A Biblical-Theological Understanding of the Covenants* (Wheaton, IL: Crossway, 2012), 524–25.

and fig tree (v. 10; cf. 1 Kings 4:25), will be restored by a greater Joshua, who will bear the people's sin once and for all, just as Exodus 28:36–38 required of the high priest.

From these two books (Jeremiah and Zechariah), we see that when the prophets promise a new and better priest, the priest envisioned is a royal priest. This furthers the picture found in David's priestly actions, and it will be supported by passages like Psalm 110 and Daniel 7:13–14, which identify the Messiah as a priest and a king. It also coheres with the kingdom of priests created by the work of this promised royal priest, a priestly people that the prophets also discuss.

A New Royal Priesthood

Isaiah 56–66 and Jeremiah 33:14–26 are two places where we find the prophets describing a future priesthood. Let's start with Isaiah, where Isaiah 53 pictures a royal servant who offers a sacrifice for the sins of his people.[18] As Peter Gentry has noted, this "Servant is not only the sacrifice, he is also the priest. . . . Moreover, he is a super-High Priest. The High Priest sprinkles only Israel, but this priest sprinkles the nations who are also included in the many."[19] As we saw in Jeremiah, it is a royal priest who will inaugurate the new covenant. And in Isaiah, it is a priestly offering that brings about a new covenant. In fact, one of the most powerful evidences of the servant's priesthood comes in the fact that the work of the servant creates a new covenant priesthood.

As many have observed, Isaiah 56–66 centers itself on this new priesthood.[20] Both Isaiah 56 and 66 present outsiders—eunuchs and Gentiles, respectively—entering the house of God to serve as priests.

---

18. The Servant Songs are four passages in Isaiah that speak of the servant of the Lord (Isa. 42:1–9; 49:1–7; 50:4–9; 52:13–53:12).

19. Peter J. Gentry, "The Atonement in Isaiah's Fourth Servant Song (Isaiah 52:13–53:12)," *Southern Baptist Journal of Theology* 11, no. 2 (2007): 43.

20. "The chiastic structure identifies Isaiah 61 . . . as the 'theological core' of Isaiah 56–66." Hank Voss, *The Priesthood of All Believers and the Missio Dei: A Canonical, Catholic, and Contextual Perspective*, Princeton Theological Monograph Series (Eugene, OR: Pickwick, 2016), 62.

Isaiah 60–62 centers the work of the Spirit on creating priests dressed in new robes of righteousness. By means of the servant's sacrifice, God is making all things new, beginning with a new family of royal priests. Thus, with new creation imagery, Isaiah 61 speaks of a new priesthood (v. 6) clothed in priestly garments (v. 10):

> Strangers shall stand and tend your flocks;
>> foreigners shall be your plowmen and vinedressers;
> *but you shall be called the priests of the LORD;*
>> they shall speak of you as the ministers of our God;
> you shall eat the wealth of the nations,
>> and in their glory you shall boast. . . .
>
> I will greatly rejoice in the LORD;
>> my soul shall exult in my God,
> for he has clothed me with the garments of salvation;
>> he has covered me with the robe of righteousness,
> as a bridegroom decks himself like a priest with a beautiful
>> headdress,
>> and as a bride adorns herself with her jewels.
>> (vv. 5–6, 10)

Priestly imagery is repeated in Isaiah 66, where the new creation speaks of priests and Levites coming from Gentile nations:

> And they shall bring all your brothers from all the nations as an offering to the LORD, on horses and in chariots and in litters and on mules and on dromedaries, to my holy mountain Jerusalem, says the LORD, just as the Israelites bring their grain offering in a clean vessel to the house of the LORD. *And some of them also I will take for priests and for Levites,* says the LORD.

For as the new heavens and the new earth
>   that I make
shall remain before me, says the LORD,
>   so shall your offspring and your name remain.
From new moon to new moon,
>   and from Sabbath to Sabbath,
all flesh shall come to worship before me,
declares the LORD. (vv. 20–23)

As Isaiah looks forward to Israel's salvation, he describes God's new covenant in priestly terms. This vision of a new creation with an international kingdom of priests promises something that far exceeds anything found in the law. Yet it is a vision that explains the priesthood of believers that comes in the New Testament when the Spirit is poured out.

Similarly, Jeremiah 33:14–26 promises priestly restoration. Only, it does so using the language of David's kingdom and the Levitical priesthood. In particular, verses 17–18 read, "For thus says the LORD: David shall never lack a man to sit on the throne of the house of Israel, and the Levitical priests shall never lack a man in my presence to offer burnt offerings, to burn grain offerings, and to make sacrifices forever." How should we understand this?

If we remember that the covenant of Levi was instituted in Numbers 25 because of the weakness of the first covenant, that will guard us from reading this as a mere return to the law. As Jeremiah looks to the future, he is not calling for a return to Sinai (see Jer. 31:32). Rather, as the promises of restoration to the nations suggest (48:47; 49:6, 39; 50:4–5; 51:6), he is looking for the redeemed of all nations (Jew and Gentile) to join in the blessings of this new covenant.

Also, if the new covenant establishes a son of David on the throne, it means that as David established priests and Levites at God's house in Jerusalem (1 Chron. 22–26), so this new David will establish a new priesthood when the temple is restored.[21] Last, when we read Jeremiah with Isaiah, we learn that Levites can come from the nations. Hence, Levites under the new covenant are not defined by their ancestry. In Isaiah this is explicit (see Isa. 66:20–21); in Jeremiah it is less so. But from all the Prophets we discover that Christ brings eunuchs and Gentiles into the house of God (Isa. 56:3–8)—an absolute impossibility under the old covenant. In this way, Jeremiah's promise of a new covenant establishes a new priesthood that will look more like Zion than Sinai.

Preparing the Way for a Royal Priest

The prophets describe not only a future priesthood but how that priesthood will arrive in time. Writing from the perspective of the exile (Ezekiel) or after the return from exile (Haggai, Zechariah, and Malachi), these prophets speak of a day when the temple, torn down in 586 BC, will be reconstructed. And with that reconstruction, there is the promise of a new priesthood. We will consider this history in the next chapter when we look at Ezra and Nehemiah, but here we should consider how the restoration of the Levitical priesthood furthers the hope of a coming royal priesthood.

For instance, Ezekiel describes the restoration of the priesthood in his day and in the days to come. First, Ezekiel 36 identifies a new priestly people. In verses 24–25 the Lord says: "I will take you from the nations and gather you from all the countries and bring you into your own land. I will sprinkle clean water on you, and you shall be clean from all your uncleannesses, and from all your idols I will cleanse you." As when the priests were purified by water for holy service (Ex. 29:4; 40:12; Lev. 8:6), this sprinkling of water suggests

---

21. In the next chapter, we will see three instances where sons of David (e.g., Jehoshaphat, Hezekiah, and Josiah) reestablish the priesthood in times of revival in Israel.

a priestly identity for God's new covenant people (cf. Heb. 10:22). The gift of the Spirit and the circumcision of the heart also indicate a people who will keep covenant with God (Ezek. 36:27). Covenant breaking is what caused Israel to lose their status as a kingdom of priests, but now with a promise of Spirit-enabled obedience, hope springs anew for an enduring covenant with a holy priesthood.

All of these promises (e.g., the cleansing, the Spirit, and the forgiveness) will be fulfilled when Christ comes, as John 3 and other passages will make use of Ezekiel to describe the identity of God's people.[22] Yet, in Ezekiel itself, we find that this promise of a new covenant, with its hope of a purified priesthood, will not come until Israel is gathered from the nations and the temple is rebuilt. This reconstruction of the temple is described in Ezekiel 40–48. It is worth noting that when the temple is rebuilt, the priesthood is restored (see 44:15–31). In Israel's history, this occurs when the exiles return from Babylon. And yet the reconstruction of the Second Temple and the return of the priests and the Levites do not solve the problems of the priesthood. A new priesthood, one wholly unlike the Levitical priesthood, will be needed, and in the final Prophets of the Old Testament we begin to see the path forward to this greater priest.

In the Twelve (Minor Prophets), Haggai, Zechariah, and Malachi form a priestly resolution to the earlier indictments of Hosea–Zephaniah.[23] Assigned to call Israel to rebuild the temple, Haggai and Zechariah are used by God to restore the temple and the Levitical priesthood to Israel in their day (cf. Ezra 6:13–15). Malachi has the final word in the Prophets, and instead of commending the reconstitution of the Levitical priesthood, he renders the most severe

---

22. Nicholas Perrin, *Jesus the Priest* (New York: SPCK, 2018), 41–44, 91, repeatedly draws from Ezek. 36 to show how this passage informs the priestly identification of Christ and his disciples.

23. Following the literary outline observed by Paul House, *The Unity of the Twelve* (Sheffield, England: Sheffield, 1990), the Twelve focus on three primary themes—sin, judgment, and restoration—with the last (restoration) being the primary focus in Haggai, Zechariah, and Malachi.

judgment. Yet he also includes the greatest promise for a purified priesthood (3:1–4). It is his final word of hope that we will consider to close this chapter.

As we observed in the last section, Malachi 1–2 condemns the manifold compromises of the Levitical priests. Yet, instead of eliminating the priesthood altogether, Malachi looks to the future purification of the priesthood:

> Behold, I send my messenger, and he will prepare the way before me. And the Lord whom you seek will suddenly come to his temple; and the messenger of the covenant in whom you delight, behold, he is coming, says the LORD of hosts. But who can endure the day of his coming, and who can stand when he appears? For he is like a refiner's fire and like fullers' soap. He will sit as a refiner and purifier of silver, and he will purify the sons of Levi and refine them like gold and silver, and they will bring offerings in righteousness to the LORD. Then the offering of Judah and Jerusalem will be pleasing to the LORD as in the days of old and as in former years. (3:1–4)

Like the other Prophets, Malachi speaks of a future when God's people are purified to serve in the presence of God. Only, in this case, Malachi supplies language quoted by the Gospels and applied directly to John the Baptist and Jesus. John, the son of a priest (Luke 1), not only prepares the way for the Lord (Mark 1:3; cf. Isa. 40:3); he prepares the way for Jesus, who is a greater priest. In Malachi, the promise of purification is presented in terms of the old covenant and the covenant with Levi. But when we turn to the New Testament, we will discover how the Gospels present Christ as greater than John, not only in his personhood but also in his priesthood.

In fact, as we finish our look at the Prophets, it is worth looking back to observe how "the prophets, by and large, see the future in priestly terms."[24] This is not always the way we think of the Prophets, and thus the focus on priesthood found here reinforces the importance of the priesthood in all Scripture. Moreover, it prepares us to understand Christ's priesthood in the New Testament. Yet, before we can go there, we need to see how the Writings confirm this priestly approach to Scripture and raise our anticipation for a priest to come from David's house.

---

24. Crispin Fletcher-Louis, "Jesus as the High Priestly Messiah (Part 1)," *Journal for the Study of the Historical Jesus* 4, no. 2 (2006): 168.

4

The Writings

The Royal Priesthood Anticipated

In the preceding chapters, we have traced the history of the priesthood from its origins in Adam, to its legislation by Moses, to its rise and fall in the Prophets. In those same Prophets, we have seen the promise of a greater royal priesthood. Now, in the Writings, we will see how these books anticipate the arrival of this royal priest. In particular, we will see from selected passages how these authors of Scripture heighten our anticipation of this royal priesthood.

While priesthood is touched on throughout the Writings, it is most prominent in 1–2 Chronicles and Ezra–Nehemiah. In these books, we find some of the most detailed descriptions of the priests. Similarly, some of the most important passages on priesthood are found in the Writings. Psalm 110, Psalms 132–34, Daniel 7:13–14, and Daniel 9:24–27 all make contributions.

In this chapter, I will survey these two books and examine these four passages.[1] By looking at these six selections, we will see how the Levitical priesthood serves the Lord in relationship to the kings of Israel. And we will also see why a priest from David's house will ultimately be needed to complete what the priests from the house of Aaron could not.

Priestly Kings and Levitical Priests in 1–2 Chronicles

To begin with, we should look at the history of priests and kings in Israel. In 1–2 Chronicles we find the same history as in 1–2 Samuel and 1–2 Kings, but it is written to a later generation of Israelites returning from exile. Written when the temple was being rebuilt, 1–2 Chronicles elevates the kingship of David's family, the central place of the temple, and the role of the priests.[2] There is good evidence for seeing the author of 1–2 Chronicles as a priest or Levite, and as we will discover, priestly themes pervade this two-part history.[3]

With respect to the priesthood, 1–2 Chronicles shows a cyclical pattern in Jerusalem. Like the check mark pattern of the priesthood (seen in the Prophets), there exists in 1–2 Chronicles a series of ups and downs, followed by greater ups and greater downs. Along the way, 1–2 Chronicles provides a history of priests in Israel that adds details to our biblical theology. In all, by looking at this history, we are better equipped to understand what kind of priesthood Jesus will bring.

A Short History of Priests and Kings

In chronological order, David brings the ark of the covenant to Jerusalem with the assistance of the Levitical priests (1 Chron. 15–16). Then he organizes the priests for service at the temple (1 Chron. 22–

---

1. I will treat Ezra–Nehemiah as one book. Though our modern Bibles separate Ezra and Nehemiah and break Chronicles into two books, the earliest manuscripts read them together. As we will see, they present a unified vision of the priests and Levites.

2. These themes are well identified in Richard Pratt, *1 & 2 Chronicles* (Fearn, Ross-shire, Scotland: Mentor, 2006), 25–36.

3. Richard Pratt, "1–2 Chronicles," in *A Biblical-Theological Introduction to the Old Testament: The Gospel Promised*, ed. Miles V. Van Pelt (Wheaton, IL: Crossway, 2016), 527.

26) and establishes Zadok as high priest (1 Chron. 29:22).[4] Solomon builds on David's foundation by constructing the temple with the wisdom God supplies (2 Chron. 1–8). Under Solomon's command, the priests are positioned to serve in the temple, where they mediate covenant relations between Yahweh and his people.[5]

After this promising start, however, the history of the priesthood begins to falter. The condition of the priesthood depends upon the faithfulness of the king. For instance, kings like Jeroboam in the North and Ahaz and Manasseh in the South lead the priests into idolatry. Subsequently, other kings, like Hezekiah and Josiah, restore the temple and the priesthood. In all, the condition of the priesthood is typically determined by the sons of David (see table 3, below).

In principle, when a faithful son of David sits on the throne, he provides for and protects Aaron's sons and God's house. By contrast, when an unfaithful son rises to power, he leads the nation and the priests to serve him, not God, with only a few historical exceptions. In short, the priests' faithfulness determines the condition of the nation, and their faithfulness is also determined by the kings. Eventually, this pattern of faithfulness, then idolatry, then temporary repentance comes to an end. After centuries of corruption and correction, God's judgment falls upon Jerusalem as both priests and kings fail to live up to God's standard (2 Chron. 36:1–16).

In all, 1–2 Chronicles records a tight relationship between the house of David and the house of Aaron. Throughout Israel's history, the works of the priests and kings mirror one another. That is to say, the Levitical priests do what priests do, and the sons of David, like David himself, are often portrayed doing priestly things—either by themselves or with the priests. In fact, by looking at two things—the

---

4. Zadok's prominence comes to the forefront in 1–2 Chronicles, as his lineage goes back to Phinehas and Eleazar—the exemplary priests of Aaron's line.

5. It should not be missed that the glory of God is so great when the temple is dedicated that the priests could not stand to minister (2 Chron. 5:14). This inability to minister stresses the greatness of God, but it may also point to the weakness of the priests. When Christ comes as the true priest, he will bring the glory of God to mankind as God the Son dwells bodily (John 1:14–18).

actions of the kings and the assignments of the Levitical priests—
we can see how kings and priests function in Israel and how their
complementary actions in the temple bless or curse the nation.

PRIESTLY KINGS

As we observed in the last chapter, 1–2 Samuel presents David as a
priestly kind of king. Chronicles repeats this image, enhances it, and
then passes it on to many of David's sons. For instance, when David
brings the ark to Jerusalem, 1 Chronicles 15:25–28 reads:

> So David and the elders of Israel and the commanders of thou-
> sands went to bring up the ark of the covenant of the LORD
> from the house of Obed-edom with rejoicing. And because
> God helped the Levites who were carrying the ark of the cove-
> nant of the LORD, they sacrificed seven bulls and seven rams.
> *David was clothed with a robe of fine linen, as also were all the*
> *Levites who were carrying the ark, and the singers and Chena-*
> *niah the leader of the music of the singers. And David wore a*
> *linen ephod.* So all Israel brought up the ark of the covenant of
> the LORD with shouting, to the sound of the horn, trumpets,
> and cymbals, and made loud music on harps and lyres.

In this priestly procession, David is robed in fine linen like the
Levites. He is also said to wear a linen ephod, which is associated
with the priests. Thus, without the text calling David a priest, his
actions are priestly. As Scott Hahn has noted, "David is described
throughout [1–2 Chronicles] in royal and priestly terms as the king
and shepherd chosen by God."[6]

Critically, David's sons are not called priests in 1–2 Chronicles,
nor do they stand at the altar and serve God in his temple. Neverthe-

---

6. Scott W. Hahn, *The Kingdom of God as Liturgical Empire: A Theological Commentary on
1–2 Chronicles* (Grand Rapids, MI: Baker Academic, 2012), 44.

less, their faithfulness is proved by their support for the priesthood and the temple. In fact, we find the sons of David regularly turning their attention to the house of God like priests (see table 3).

Table 3. A history of David's faithful sons and priestly service

King (Chapters)	Build/ Cleanse the House	Offer Sacrifice	Receive/ Renew Covenant	Organize Priests	Offer Prayer / Pronounce Blessing
David (1 Chron. 10-29)	1 Chron. 21:18-30; 22:1-19; 29:1-9	1 Sam. 24:18-25; 2 Chron. 3:1	1 Chron. 17:1-15	1 Chron. 23-26	1 Chron. 17:16-27; 29:10-22
Solomon (2 Chron. 1-9)	2 Chron. 2:1-5:14	2 Chron. 7:5, 7-10		2 Chron. 5:2-14; 7:6	2 Chron. 6:1-42
Asa* (2 Chron. 14-16)	2 Chron. 15:8	2 Chron. 15:9-11	2 Chron. 15:12-15		
Jehosha-phat (2 Chron. 17-20)	2 Chron. 20:5†			2 Chron. 17:7-9; 19:8-11	2 Chron. 20:6-23
Jehoiada (2 Chron. 23-24)			2 Chron. 23:16	2 Chron. 23:1-11	
Joash (2 Chron. 23-24)	2 Chron. 24:4, 8-13	2 Chron. 24:14		2 Chron. 24:5-7	NA‡
Heze-kiah** (2 Chron. 29-31)	2 Chron. 29:3-19	2 Chron. 29:20-36; 30:1-27	2 Chron. 29:10	2 Chron. 31:2-21	cf. 2 Kings 19:14-19
Manasseh (2 Chron. 33)					2 Chron. 33:10-16
Josiah (2 Chron. 34-35)	2 Chron. 34:1-7, 9	2 Chron. 35:7-9	2 Chron. 34:30-32	2 Chron. 35:2-18	

* Beginning with Asa, each of David's righteous sons reigns after a period of unfaithfulness in David's house.
† Second Chronicles does not record Jehoshaphat's work on the house, but a "new court" indicates some care for the house of God.
‡ The absence of prayer corresponds to the underlying wickedness of Joash (2 Chron. 24:17-18).
** Hezekiah is a son of David, but also a son of Aaron. His mother was a daughter of the priest Joash (2 Chron. 24:20; 26:5).

From the lives of David and his sons, we learn how the kings consecrate God's house, offer sacrifices, and teach the people. In practice, David and his sons assemble the priests to carry out these duties. Such priestly administration is suggestive that the kings act like priests, for previously organization of the priests was assigned to Ithamar and Eleazar, two of Aaron's sons (see Ex. 38:21; Num. 3:32; 4:28, 33). At the same time, there are many instances when the kings do not delegate priestly actions; they actually join in the work. For example, David wears the priestly ephod as he brings the ark to Jerusalem (1 Chron. 15:27). Solomon pronounces a blessing on the people (2 Chron. 6:1–42). Asa repairs the altar (2 Chron. 15:8). Jehoshaphat intercedes for the people (2 Chron. 20:6–23). Hezekiah mediates a covenant renewal (2 Chron. 29:10). And Josiah leads the nation to keep Passover (2 Chron. 35:1) after finding the book of the law in the temple (2 Chron. 34:14–21). Individually, any one of these actions might not signify a trend, but together they represent a pattern in 1–2 Chronicles—the sons of David act like priests.

Certainly, these sons of David have not replaced the Levitical priests, as we will see below. However, in building altars, guarding God's house, and leading God's people to do what the law requires, the priestly commitments of David's house are considerable. From another angle, zeal for God's house and God's covenant proves David and his faithful sons are not like the kings of other nations. They are men after God's own heart—that is, their faithfulness centers on their patronage and protection of the temple and the priesthood. In fact, it is only when David and his sons act like pagan kings that they invite God's judgment. By contrast, when David's sons act like priests, they fulfill their true calling and bring blessing to the nation.

The Levitical Priesthood

In 1–2 Chronicles we also see how the priests and Levites serve the Lord and his people. As 1 Chronicles 16:39–40 says,

> [David] left Zadok the priest and his brothers the priests before the tabernacle of the LORD in the high place that was at Gibeon to offer burnt offerings to the LORD on the altar of burnt offering regularly morning and evening, to do all that is written in the Law of the LORD that he commanded Israel.

Expanding on this statement of obedience, 1–2 Chronicles gives a composite of the priesthood, where everything commanded by the law is obeyed at one time or another. To survey the whole history of Israel: The priests draw near to God (2 Chron. 29:11; 35:2; cf. Ex. 28:1). They mix the incense (1 Chron. 9:30–32; cf. Ex. 30:22–38), carry the ark (1 Chron. 15:11–14; 2 Chron. 5:5–7; cf. Num. 3; Josh. 3–6), blow the trumpets (1 Chron. 15:24; 16:6; 2 Chron. 7:6; 13:14; cf. Num. 10:1–10), offer sacrifices (1 Chron. 16:39–40; 2 Chron. 13:11–12; 30:1–27; 35:7–9; cf. Lev. 1–7), and teach the people God's law (2 Chron. 17:7–9; 31:4; cf. Lev. 10:11).[7] As an extension of their teaching, the priests also decide legal cases in Jerusalem (2 Chron. 19:8–11; cf. Deut. 17:8–13).[8]

Generally speaking, the priests carry out the righteous (and sometimes unrighteous) desires of the king and the plans for temple

---

7. In some cases, they also receive a rebuke for failing to teach God's law (2 Chron. 15:3). This reveals the ongoing need for their teaching ministry.

8. In many of these instances—e.g., mixing incense (1 Chron. 9:30–31), carrying the ark (1 Chron. 15:11–14; 2 Chron. 5:5–7), deciding legal matters (2 Chron. 19:8)—the priests receive assistance from the Levites. In other instances, the priests and Levites serve side by side in their service in the temple (e.g., 2 Chron. 5:12–14; 29:34). One might conclude from these moments of mutual service that the distinction between priests and Levites has been dissolved. Yet this would be an incomplete picture, for we regularly see priests distinguished from the Levites (e.g., 1 Chron. 9:2, 10–27; 15:11–12; 23:2; 24:31; 28:21; 2 Chron. 7:6; 8:14–15; 23:4; 31:2; 35:10). Indeed, when the Levitical priesthood serve faithfully, they are the ones who maintain the holy boundaries of God. This includes maintaining the distinction between priests and Levites.

worship. At other times, the priests stand up and oppose the evil actions of the throne. For instance, Jehoiada leads the priests and Levites to oppose the evil queen Athalia (2 Chron. 23). Later, Azariah and eighty priests remove Uzziah from the altar of incense when the king brazenly attempts to approach God without authorization (2 Chron. 26). This discipline of Uzziah suggests that David and his sons could offer sacrifices to (re)dedicate the temple for service, something many sons of David do.[9] But they do not possess the right to draw near in the house of God as priests; this was the error of Uzziah.

In the end, 1–2 Chronicles shows how the priesthood legislated in the Pentateuch works in the history of Israel. While we saw the compromise of the priesthood in the Prophets, 1–2 Chronicles gives us the details of how priests and kings related to one another. At times, when righteous kings rule in Jerusalem, they build or rededicate the temple and set priests in place to serve the Lord. At other times, unrighteous kings twist the priesthood to their own ends, which results in corruption. Ultimately, this priestly pattern of faithfulness and idolatry comes to an end when God brings judgment on Jerusalem. As 2 Chronicles 36:14–16 says:

> All the officers of the priests and the people likewise were exceedingly unfaithful, following all the abominations of the nations. And they polluted the house of the LORD that he had made holy in Jerusalem.
>
> The LORD, the God of their fathers, sent persistently to them by his messengers, because he had compassion on his people and on his dwelling place. But they kept mocking the messengers of God, despising his words and scoffing at his

---

9. See 1 Chron. 21:18–30; 22:1–19; 29:1–9; 2 Chron. 2:1–5:14; 15:8; 20:5; 24:4, 8–13; 29:3–19; 34:1–7, 9.

> prophets, until the wrath of the LORD rose against his people, until there was no remedy.

These words explain why Israel goes into exile: the priests and the people have been exceedingly unfaithful, they have refused to listen to God's word (as written down by Moses and repeated by the prophets), and they have ultimately defiled God's house.

As 1–2 Chronicles ends, we are confronted with the same truth found in the Prophets: the Levitical priesthood is not able to bring lasting salvation. For generations, the righteous sons of David have assembled and assigned the Levitical priests to lead the nation in worship. Many times, these kings have led lavish rededication services to reopen the temple.[10] Still, Israel's law and its priests can never achieve the redemption God will bring in Christ. Ultimately, the Levitical priesthood will need to be replaced by a greater priesthood. Psalm 110 makes this point explicit, but before turning there we need to see what happens when Israel returns from exile.

The Restoration of the Priests in Ezra–Nehemiah

Ezra–Nehemiah is perhaps the mostly priestly book in the Writings. In twenty-three chapters, "priest(s)" is used seventy times, "Levite(s)" sixty-five. Not including the six lists of priests and Levites,[11] Ezra–Nehemiah consistently puts "the priests and the Levites" together.[12]

---

10. Examples of "once-for-all" dedication sacrifices for the temple include those of David (1 Chron. 22:1–19; 29:1–9), Solomon (2 Chron. 7:5, 7–10), Asa (2 Chron. 15:9–11), Joash (2 Chron. 24:14), Hezekiah (2 Chron. 29:20–36; 30:1–27), and Josiah (2 Chron. 35:7–9).

11. Ezra 2:36–42; 10:18–24; Neh. 7:39–45; 10:1–26; 11:10–19; 12:1–26. These lists also include temple servants (Ezra 2:43–54; Neh. 7:46–56; 11:21), the sons of Solomon's servants (Ezra 2:55–57; Neh. 7:57–60), and gatekeepers, overseers, and singers (Neh. 11:19–24). Priests and Levites are also listed in the rebuilders of the city wall in Neh. 3:1, 17, 20, 28.

12. E.g., Ezra 1:5; 2:70; 3:8–12; 6:16, 20; 7:7, 13; 8:29–30, 33; 9:1; 10:5; Neh. 8:9, 13; 9:38; 10:28, 34, 38; 11:3, 20; 12:1, 30, 44; 13:29–30. Illustrating the relationship between priests and Levites, when Ezra reads the Law, the Levites join him to teach the people (Neh. 8:7, 9, 11, 13). Likewise, as they continue to read the Law (Neh. 9:3), the Levites stand on the steps crying out (9:4) and blessing God (9:5). The complete picture is one where "Ezra the priest" (8:2, 9) leads the assembly, assisted by the Levites.

Echoing the Pentateuch, a distinction between priests and Levites remains after the exile. The priests serve at the altar (Ezra 3:1–7; 7:17; cf. Neh. 10:34); the Levites serve as guardians to God's house (Neh. 7:1; cf. Ezra 2:40–42, 70; 7:7; Neh. 7:43–45; 10:9–24, 39; 11:15–24). Throughout, Levites are presented as assistants to Aaron's sons (Neh. 10:38; 12:47) and as mediators going between the priests and the people (Neh. 8:13–18; 10:35–39; 12:47).[13]

Moving beyond the titles, Ezra–Nehemiah records the reconstruction of the altar, the temple, and the city of Jerusalem—all of which depend on the ministry of the Levitical priesthood. In particular, we see Ezra the priest giving himself to studying the law so that he can teach it (Ezra 7:10). Nehemiah records Ezra reading the law to the people (8:3) and leading the people to understand it (8:1–8). In this way, his priestly priorities are shared with the whole nation, and with the help of other priests and Levites, he brings spiritual revival to Jerusalem. Ezra 9 records his prayer of confession, which prompts a whole nation to confess their covenant unfaithfulness (Ezra 10). In this same chapter, Ezra initiates a covenant renewal (10:3). All in all, Ezra exemplifies what a priest should look like. Through his model and his appointment of others (7:15; 8:24; cf. Neh. 12:44–47), we see that priests protect God's Holy Place, teach God's law, offer sacrifices, make confession, and lead the congregation in worship (see table 4).[14]

Nehemiah also relies on the priests (e.g., 7:1; 12:31, 44–47; 13:13–14), and in the book bearing his name we see how the priests enable God's people to worship again. Still, two points should be noted. First, the glory of God never fills the second temple like it did the tabernacle (Ex. 40) and Solomon's temple (1 Kings 8:11; 2 Chron. 5:14). This indicates the

---

13. E.g., the Levites are the ones who take the word of God from Ezra the priest to the people (Neh. 8:13–18), and the Levites are the ones who bring the people's tithes into the house of God (Neh. 10:35–39).

14. The addition of praise and worship came to the Levites in the times of David and the Jerusalem temple.

incomplete nature of the return from exile. Second, Ezra and Nehemiah both end like 1–2 Chronicles. Many of the priests defile themselves by marrying foreign women (see Ezra 10:18–24; Neh. 13:23–29), and in both instances Ezra and Nehemiah must reprove the priests sternly. With tragic irony, what set Phinehas apart in Numbers 25 and led to God's covenant with Levi—namely, Phinehas's zeal against the sexual immorality of Israel—is reversed here. And though Ezra and Nehemiah attend to the failures of the priests, Nehemiah 13:29–30 indicates the need to cleanse the priesthood from its desecration once again.

Table 4. The role of priests and Levites in Ezra–Nehemiah

	Guarding	**Teaching**	**Offering Sacrifices, Prayers, and Praise**
Ezra	Priests are guarded from receiving unregistered priests (2:61–63). Priests and Levites guard the offerings (8:24–30).*	Ezra the priest studies, applies, and teaches the law (7:10). Ezra recruits Levites to go with him back to Israel (8:15–20).	Priests restore the altar (3:1–7; cf. 6:3, 10). Priests blow trumpets; Levites lead in song (3:10–11). Priests and Levites celebrate the Passover (6:19–22). Priests offer evening sacrifice (9:4–5; cf. Ex. 29:39–41).
Nehemiah	Gatekeepers are associated with the Levites (e.g., 7:1–3, 73; 10:28; cf. Ezra 2:70; 7:7). Levites guard God's holy city as gatekeepers (7:1; cf. Ps. 84:10).†	Ezra is joined by the Levites when he teaches (8:1–12). Ezra trains and sends Levites to organize the Feast of Booths (8:13–18).	Princes, Levites, and priests make confession (9:1–38); Levites cry out in the temple (9:4–5). Priests offer "great sacrifices" (12:43) when the wall is dedicated. (Levitical?) singers continue to bless God in worship services (12:31, 36, 38–43, 45–46).‡

* This Levitical security detail matches the caravan of priests and Levites that stood guard around the tabernacle (see Num. 3).
† Gatekeepers are mentioned fourteen times in Ezra–Nehemiah (Ezra 2:42, 70; 7:7; 10:24; Neh. 7:1, 45, 73; 10:28, 39; 11:19; 12:25, 45, 47; 13:5).
‡ Singers are mentioned twenty-three times in Ezra–Nehemiah, usually in conjunction with the Levites, gatekeepers, and temple servants. Based on Neh. 12:45 we have good reason to believe these singers are a class of Levites (cf. 1 Chron. 25–26).

In Ezra–Nehemiah, the leaders of the nation intervene to purify the priesthood, but once again the weakness of the Levitical priesthood is displayed. What Israel (and the world) needs is a new priesthood, one that transcends in power and provision the weakness of Aaron and his sons. Already we have seen that this better priesthood is associated with David and his royal sons, and now we are ready to see that promise in its most explicit form.

A Royal Priest like Melchizedek (Ps. 110)

Psalm 110 is the most important passage in the Old Testament for understanding the purposes of the priesthood, as well as being the most quoted psalm in the New Testament. With respect to priesthood, Psalm 110 contains the most important verse for understanding how Jesus, as a son of David, could be a priest. And with respect to its citation in the New Testament, its application to Christ's ascension (v. 1) and his priestly ministry (v. 4) are vital for understanding how the apostles understand the person and work of Christ.

Indeed, as we have noted throughout this book, priests and kings are separate-but-related offices in Israel. In Adam, royal and priestly actions were unified in the first son of God; in Israel, the nation was called to be a kingdom of priests; and in David and his sons, we have seen royal and priestly themes overlap from one generation to the next. Now, in Psalm 110, as David looks to the future, he sees that his Lord is both a king and a priest. Even more, making a connection with the priest-king of Salem, David identifies his Lord as a "priest forever after the order of Melchizedek" (v. 4). Here is the full text of this pivotal psalm.

A Psalm of David.

The Lord says to my Lord:
 "Sit at my right hand,
until I make your enemies your footstool."

The LORD sends forth from Zion
>   your mighty scepter.
>   Rule in the midst of your enemies!
Your people will offer themselves freely
>   on the day of your power,
>   in holy garments;
from the womb of the morning,
>   the dew of your youth will be yours.
The LORD has sworn
>   and will not change his mind,
"You are a priest forever
>   after the order of Melchizedek."

The Lord is at your right hand;
>   he will shatter kings on the day of his wrath.
He will execute judgment among the nations,
>   filling them with corpses;
he will shatter chiefs
>   over the wide earth.
He will drink from the brook by the way;
>   therefore he will lift up his head.

Psalm 110 records two statements from God (vv. 1, 4), followed by two corresponding explanations (vv. 2–3, 5–7). In expansion of verse 1, verses 2–3 detail the way God will give the king a people clothed in priestly apparel (cf. Pss. 68:18; 132:9).[15] Likewise, 110:4 is followed by God's holy judgment on his enemies through this royal priest (vv. 5–7; cf. Pss. 2:1–3; 68:14; 138–45). In this way, Psalm 110 records a royal (v. 1) and priestly (v. 4) word to the greater son of David.[16]

---

15. Though Ps. 110:3 is a highly debated verse, "holy garments" (or "holy mountains"—ESV margin) have priestly connotations. The image of people freely coming to Zion also recalls the way Levites were given to Aaron (Num. 3:9; 8:19; 18:6; cf. Ps. 68:18; Eph. 4:8).

16. For application of v. 1, see Matt. 22:44; Mark 12:36; Luke 20:42–43; Acts 2:34–35; for v. 4, see Heb. 5:6; 7:17, 21.

Focusing on this psalm by itself, we might only get a vision of military glory. Yet, when we read Psalm 110 with the rest of book 5 (Pss. 107–50), we discover how these psalms outline the elements of Christ's royal priesthood. Set in a context of a new exodus, where God gathers his people from various places of peril (Ps. 107), Psalm 110 answers a cry for salvation to come from God's right hand (Pss. 108:6; 109:31; 110:4–5). Then, following Psalm 110, there is a path of salvation that leads from Psalm 110 to seven psalms of praise (Pss. 111–17), a new sacrifice (Ps. 118), a new law (Ps. 119), a new temple with a new priesthood (Pss. 120–34), renewed worship (Pss. 135–37), and a new spiritual battle with seven psalms of David (Pss. 138–45). Finally, this progression culminates in cosmic praise (Pss. 146–50).

More specifically, Psalm 110 should be read with Psalm 118 to understand how David's Lord will defeat his enemies.[17] He will not simply strike down the nations, as Psalm 110, read by itself, might suggest. Rather, as the stone rejected by the builders, he will be forsaken (v. 22), even bound to the altar as the festal sacrifice (vv. 26–27). Through this offering, Jesus will become an atoning sacrifice for the sins of his people. At the same time, he will be given authority to sit at God's right hand (v. 1), which enables him to wage spiritual warfare on the earth—saving his elect and judging his enemies. Such a vision complements what we have seen in the prophets (e.g., Jer. 30:21; Zech. 3:1–10; 6:9–15)—a priest from the house of David who will create a new kingdom of priests when he comes.[18]

---

17. In the Gospels, we see how Jesus cites Pss. 110 and 118 to contest the accusations of the scribes and the Pharisees. His use of these two psalms in Matt. 21–22 gives us warrant for reading them together, as does the shared imagery of God's right hand expressed in both (Pss. 110:1, 5; 118:15–16).

18. On the priestly functions of this Davidic king in the Psalms, see Willem VanGemeren, "Psalms," in *The Expositor's Bible Commentary*, ed. Frank E. Gaebelein, vol. 5 (Grand Rapids, MI: Zondervan, 1991), 586–91.

A Priesthood Given to David's Lord (Pss. 132–34)

Psalms 132–34 go further to explain how this coming royal priest will bring a new priesthood. Standing at the end of the Psalms of Ascent, Psalm 132 says of the greater David that he will be joined by many sons on his throne (v. 12).[19] This mention of "throne" links Psalm 110:1 and Psalm 132:11–12, as does Yahweh swearing a "sure oath" to David (132:11) and choosing Zion (Jerusalem) as his place of priestly service (132:13, 16). In keeping with Psalm 110, therefore, the qualification for priesthood in Psalm 132 is being clothed with righteousness (v. 9) and salvation (v. 16), not Levitical heritage.[20] In this way, we see how the new covenant will not restore the priesthood to Levi; it will enlarge the priesthood to all those who take refuge in the true royal priest.[21]

Because of the greater priesthood of David's Lord, all those who trust in him will be made priests in his kingdom. Indeed, just as priesthood began in the Old Testament as a family affair, so it will be in Christ (cf. Mark 3:31–35). Only, as the New Testament will confirm, new covenant priests will stand in God's house because Jesus has brought them near, not because of their Levitical heritage. When Christ comes as the greater priest, the Levitical priesthood will be surpassed by a kingdom of priests that will come with the power of the Holy Spirit. We are getting ahead of ourselves, but that's the whole point of the Psalms—to stir up longings for this coming royal priest!

19. Solomon's psalm about God's house (Ps. 127) stands at the center of Pss. 120–34. See O. Palmer Robertson, *The Flow of the Psalms: Discovering Their Structure and Theology* (Phillipsburg, NJ: P&R, 2015), 210–17, who also notes how Aaron's priestly blessing (Num. 6:24–26) plays a formative role in the Songs of Ascent.

20. It is worth observing that Solomon prays for the priests to be "clothed with salvation" when he dedicates the temple (2 Chron. 6:41).

21. Following suit, Pss. 133 and 134 promise a blessed priesthood. Whereas Israel's blessings depended on the faithfulness of Aaron and his sons, the new priesthood of David's righteous son (Ps. 110) will secure blessing for his brothers (Ps. 133)—unity (v. 1), anointing (v. 2), and "life forevermore" (v. 3). Indeed, when we read Pss. 132–34 in light of the New Testament, it is difficult to conceive of a more glorious passage.

The Son of Man: A King Who Draws Near (Dan. 7:13–14)

In the book of Daniel royal priesthood continues to take center stage. As Daniel identifies the rule of Yahweh over the nations, Daniel also "uses cultic language to describe these cultic elements and thereby links his book to the priestly traditions."[22] This combination of royal and priestly themes matches what we have seen already, and in Daniel we discover two places where royal priesthood comes to the foreground. The first is Daniel 7:13–14; the second is Daniel 9:24–27.

Daniel 7 is a key passage for differentiating two kinds of kingdoms—beastly kingdoms, which rule with greed, avarice, and slavery, versus a human(e) kingdom ruled by a Son of Man who will defeat evil and bring peace. Verses 13–14 record:

I saw in the night visions,

> and behold, with the clouds of heaven
>> there came one like a son of man,
> and he came to the Ancient of Days
>> and was presented before him.
> And to him was given dominion
>> and glory and a kingdom,
> that all peoples, nations, and languages
>> should serve him;
> his dominion is an everlasting dominion,
>> which shall not pass away,
> and his kingdom one
>> that shall not be destroyed.

Set against the four beasts (vv. 1–8), this "one like a son of man" is presented as a new Adam who will receive authority over all nations

---

22. Winfried Vogel, *The Cultic Motif in the Book of Daniel* (New York: Peter Lang, 2010), 15.

because of his inherent righteousness (not violent force). Importantly, the imagery of this figure is suggestive of multiple passages in the Old Testament—all of which recall "sons" who have been presented as royal priests. Adam, Abraham, and David come to mind, but it is Aaron who will receive our focus.

On the Day of Atonement, the law required the high priest to purify God's mercy seat, so that Yahweh would continue to dwell with and bless the nation of Israel. Importantly, Leviticus 16 speaks of the cloud of incense covering this mercy seat (vv. 2, 13). Recalling this imagery, Daniel describes how the Son of Man is to approach God's throne.[23] Daniel 7:13 says he "was presented" before the Ancient of Days, just as Aaron was commanded to "present" himself before God on the Day of Atonement (Lev. 16:6, 9, 11). Indeed, when we read Daniel 7:13–14 with Leviticus 16, which describes the Day of Atonement, we see priestly elements in the one who is like a son of man.[24]

As he receives authority from God in Daniel 7:14, the Son of Man is presented as royal. It is important to see the priestly approach of this Son of Man prior to this bestowal of power. As with all true priests, the Son of Man does not assert himself, as the beastly kings of the nations do. Rather, like the prince of Jeremiah 30:21, he is invited by the Ancient of Days to approach the throne of God, which he does "on the clouds." This reference shares a striking resemblance to the priest on the Day of Atonement, who is invited by God to draw near with the clouds of incense. And in the dominion that is offered to the Son of Man, there is a strong connection with Adam. Thus, with Aaron and Adam in view, these verses are suggestive of a royal priest.

---

23. At this point, it may be helpful to recall how Aaron himself is portrayed like Adam in Ex. 28.

24. For a priestly reading of Dan. 7:13–14, see the illuminating work of Nicholas Perrin, *Jesus the Priest* (New York: SPCK, 2018), 169–79.

The Prince Offers a New Covenant Sacrifice (Dan. 9:24–27)

Daniel 9:24–27 presents another portrait of a royal priest who will establish a "strong covenant with many for one week" (v. 27). The statement regarding "one week" brings up the notoriously difficult interpretation of the seventy weeks.[25] However, if we can focus on the anointed "prince/leader" who will bring blessing to his people and justice to the world (v. 25) and who will be cut off on behalf of his people (v. 26), we are in a good position to understand how the covenant is strengthened by this individual (v. 27). Reading verses 26–27 together, we find that they "describe the work of the Messiah," who is a royal figure (a prince), "dying vicariously to uphold a covenant with many and to deal decisively with sin, thus ending the sacrificial system."[26]

Remembering how Jeremiah informs Daniel (see Dan. 9:1–2), we might interpret this substitutionary sacrifice and strong covenant in terms that echo Jeremiah. As we observed in the last chapter, Jeremiah tells us that a royal "prince" will establish the new covenant (31:31–34) by means of his priestly service (30:21). Similarly, in Daniel the prince is "cut off, *but not for himself.* The coming king will give his life to deliver his people."[27] In this way, Daniel 9 presents a righteous king who does not oppress the nations like the beastly rulers of Daniel 7–12. Rather, he offers himself up as a priestly sacrifice for the salvation of his people. Therefore, his kingdom will be given to those who suffer with the Son of Man (7:18), and even if they are put to death, they will shine with the light of God's glory (12:2–3).

This is why the covenant he establishes is secure—not even death can defeat it. And though the full meaning of this promise awaits the

---

25. In what follows, I will follow Peter Gentry's approach to Dan. 9. Peter J. Gentry and Stephen J. Wellum, *Kingdom through Covenant: A Biblical-Theological Understanding of the Covenants* (Wheaton, IL: Crossway, 2012), 531–64.

26. Gentry and Wellum, *Kingdom through Covenant*, 547.

27. Gentry and Wellum, *Kingdom through Covenant*, 543.

arrival of the Son of Man, who is the prince who will be cut off for his people, we can see how Daniel raises our anticipation for the coming royal priest. With Psalms 110 and 132 and the rest of the Writings, these two passages clarify and amplify our hopes for a royal priesthood. And now we are ready to see the royal priest of whom all the Law, the Prophets, and the Writings are speaking.

5

The Gospels

The Royal Priesthood Arrives

Every time the president of the United States changes, so does the presidential furniture. As the new president is sworn in on the Capitol steps, the White House undergoes the world's fastest interior redecoration. Within hours, the material possessions of the outgoing president are packed up and sent out, and the furnishings of the new president are brought in and unpacked.

In America this peaceful exchange of power has happened over forty times, but few transitions of power are made with such peace. In our fallen world, earthly rulers violently oppose those who threaten them. The same is true in the Bible. When Jesus brings his Father's kingdom to earth, Roman rulers and Jewish priests conspire against him. From his birth to his death, the leaders in Jerusalem oppose God's Messiah, and instead of welcoming the one to whom the law pointed, they reject God's Son to preserve their own glory. Capturing this spiritual warfare, the Gospels tell a story of two priesthoods.

Like the Old Testament prophets who indicted the priests, Jesus comes denouncing the priests of Jerusalem—a prophetic action that will set his priesthood against theirs. At the same time, the Gospels report how the priests "sacrifice" the Lamb of God to preserve their nation. By crucifying Jesus, the priests seal their own judgment, even as Jesus's obedience unto death proves his superlative priesthood. Yet, what the priests intend for evil, God intends for good—namely, the appointment of Jesus to God's right hand as the long-awaited royal priest.

Still, for all the ways priesthood is mentioned in the Bible, many Christians devote little attention to Christ's priesthood *in the Gospels*. Few deny his priesthood in general; Hebrews makes clear that Jesus is a great high priest. But many miss the way Matthew, Mark, Luke, and John present his royal priesthood. This is understandable but unfortunate. It is understandable because the Gospels never label Jesus a priest, but it is unfortunate because it misses a major feature of Christ's glory. As we have seen with Adam, Abraham, Moses, and even David, God's priests are not always identified by title. Often their priesthood is observed through their actions. This is how we will approach the priesthood of Christ in the Gospels.

Seeing Christ's Priesthood in the Gospels

By the numbers, the Gospels mention (high) priesthood ninety-six times, but in every instance the sons of Aaron are in view.[1] Yet, if

---

1. Borrowing a portion of Albert Vanhoye's illuminating chart, we can see how often terms like "priest," "high priest," and "priesthood" are used. Vanhoye, *Old Testament Priests and the New Priest: According to the New Testament*, trans. J. Bernard Orchard (Petersham, MA: St. Bede's, 1986), 63.

	Matthew	Mark	Luke	John
Priest	3	2	5	1
High priest	25	22	15	21
Priesthood				1
To exercise priesthood			1	

we remember that true priests never volunteer for service, it makes sense that Jesus does not call himself a priest.[2] Rather, if we see how the Gospel writers take their cues from the terminology and types of the Old Testament, we have good reason to see Christ's priesthood through what he does and, in the case of his birth and baptism, what is said and done to him. Indeed, from the first historical event in the Gospels (Zechariah the priest offering incense in the temple in Luke 1:8–9) to the last (Christ raising his hands like a priest to bless his people in Luke 24:50–51), priesthood is present. And in between these priestly bookends, the Gospels are filled with episodes that point to Jesus's priestly actions.

In this chapter, I will trace his priesthood along the lines of the priestly definition I have employed throughout. Through actions that (1) *sanctify* God's place and God's people, (2) *sacrifice* God's offerings, and (3) *speak* God's covenant, we will witness Jesus's priesthood. Additionally, we will see how Jesus's birth story and baptism identify Jesus as a priest.

Jesus's Birth and Baptism Introduce Us to Jesus the Priest

Before looking directly at the priestly actions of Jesus, we should notice how the Gospels introduce him in priestly ways. For instance, Luke's Gospel begins with the birth narratives of John the Baptist and Jesus. In my family, these two chapters bring back memories of Christmas morning and reading Luke's Gospel in our living room. Such an association between Luke 1–2 and Christmas may cause us to miss what Luke is highlighting. If we can approach Luke with new eyes, however, we discover that he focuses

---

2. Another reason Jesus cannot be declared an official priest in the Gospels is that prior to his death and resurrection, the law of Moses and the Levitical priesthood are in force. In obedience to the law, Jesus cannot be priest. Yet, in obedience to the eternal purposes of God, to which the law was but one part in the plan, Jesus comes not to rehabilitate the Levitical priesthood but to replace it.

on Christ's priesthood through the unique relationship between John the Baptist and Jesus.

Immediately, Luke opens his Gospel in the temple. As if filming a compelling screenplay, the camera pans to Zechariah, a priest from Aaron's house, offering incense at the altar (Luke 1:5–23). In these verses, at least six clues put the priesthood before us:

1. Zechariah is identified as a "priest" (Luke 1:5a; cf. vv. 8–9).

2. Zechariah's wife is from the tribe of Aaron (v. 5b), her name, Elizabeth, recalling Aaron's wife Elisheba (Ex. 6:23).

3. Zechariah's name reminds us of the prophet-priest Zechariah, whose night visions promised the restoration of Israel through a royal priest (Zech. 3:1–10; 6:9–15).

4. Elizabeth's barrenness harkens back to Hannah, the mother of Samuel—another priestly figure.

5. The angel's promise of a son to Zechariah introduces John as another priest in the story of redemption (Luke 1:8–17). Like Samuel, John will be used by God to prepare the way for a Davidic king (see Luke 1:67–80).

6. The citation from Malachi 4:5–6 in Luke 1:16–17 picks up the promise that God will purify the Levites when he brings a new messenger of the covenant (Mal. 2–4).

With these clues, Luke points to the temple and the priests who serve there. Yet, as Zechariah will prophesy, it is not his son who will restore the hopes of Israel (Luke 1:67–79) but another Joshua (Jesus)—like the one foretold by an earlier Zechariah (Zech. 3:1–10)!

Like Zechariah the prophet, John's father states that "a horn of salvation for us" will arise from the "house of his servant David" (Luke 1:69). John will be "prophet of the Most High" and the one who "will go before the Lord to prepare his ways" (Luke 1:76).[3] Ironically, the son born to the Levitical priest will not serve in the temple; instead he will end up in the wilderness (Luke 1:80). By contrast, Jesus, who is born in Bethlehem, is presented in the temple (Luke 2:22–38). Later, while still a boy, Jesus will call the temple his Father's house (2:49). This focus on the temple recalls the kind of priestly actions we saw in David, and in Luke's Gospel we can note five ways Luke introduces Jesus as a royal priest.[4]

First, multiple allusions to 1 Samuel 1–2 identify a change in the priesthood. In 1 Samuel the sins of Israel's priests (Eli and his sons) prompted their removal and the promise of a new priesthood (2:35). Recalling this previous change, Luke begins his Gospel with many allusions to 1 Samuel. For instance, Mary's Magnificat (Luke 1:46–56) echoes in form and content Hannah's prayer (1 Sam. 2:1–10). Then it says of John the Baptist that he "grew up and became strong in spirit" (Luke 1:80), just like Samuel (1 Sam. 2:26; 3:19). Most importantly, though, "God's purpose in Samuel was to cut the corrupt line of Eli, Hophni, and Phinehas, and raise up 'a faithful priest who will do according to what is in My heart and in My soul.'"[5] In 1 Samuel, Hannah bore a son who would prepare the way for David, Israel's priestly king. In Luke, this promise has been fulfilled to its greatest degree, as John the Baptist comes to prepare the way for Jesus, who will be the king and priest foretold in 1 Samuel 2:35.

Second, Jesus eclipses John and his priestly house. With a focus on the priestly line of Aaron (vv. 5–25) and the royal house of David

---

3. John's role as a prophet does not deny his priestly status. In the Old Testament, Jeremiah and Ezekiel both came from priestly families.

4. Many of these observations, as well as the ones that follow, are suggested by Peter J. Leithart, *The Priesthood of the Plebs: A Theology of Baptism* (Eugene, OR: Wipf & Stock, 2003), 111–20.

5. Leithart, *The Priesthood of the Plebs*, 114.

(vv. 26–45), Luke fills his first chapter with names and places associated with priests. By comparison between the placement of Zechariah (in the temple) and John (in the wilderness) (see vv. 5, 80), Luke juxtaposes Aaron's movement away from the temple toward the wilderness with Jesus's movement from Bethlehem to the courts of God's house (2:1–52). In particular, Luke identifies Jesus as Mary's "firstborn" (2:7), a designation that recalls the special place of firstborns in Israel.

In fact, when Mary presents Jesus at the temple, like Hannah did Samuel (1 Sam. 1:24), Luke states, "as it is written in the Law of the Lord, 'Every male who first opens the womb shall be called holy to the Lord'" (Luke 2:23). This Old Testament reference combines the redemption price of the firstborn (Ex. 13:2, 12–13; Num. 3:41–51; 18:15–16) with the priestly title "holy to the Lord" (Ex. 28:36).[6] Together, this would make Jesus a firstborn who would redeem the Levites, reversing the effects of Sinai, where the Levites took the place of firstborn sons (see Ex. 32:25–29). Whereas the Levites replaced the firstborns to assist the priests under the law (Num. 3:40–51), now in Christ a whole new order is dawning.

Luke further explains the relationship between Jesus and John the Baptist by citing Malachi (Luke 1:17, 76; 3:4). Fulfilling Malachi 3:1–4, God's messenger prepares the way for the Lord to enter his temple, while the "messenger of the [new] covenant" enters the temple to purify the Levites. Luke picks up this promise and shows how John's wilderness ministry prepares the way for Christ. With great effect, this temple-to-wilderness reversal illustrates the words of Mary (1:46–56) and anticipates the ministries of John and Jesus (cf. John 3:30).

Third, Jesus's baptism identifies his priestly service. As a part of their consecration for service in God's house, priests had to be

---

6. Credit to Peter Gentry and Seth Leeman for alerting me to this point.

washed with water (Ex. 29:4; 40:12; Lev. 8:6). Now, as Jesus embarks on his earthly service to God, he too is washed with water (i.e., baptized). While many ritual washings have been suggested as the background to John's baptism, "all evidence in Second-Temple Judaism points to Jewish ritual bathing practices' being self-administered."[7] Only the priestly consecration involved one person "baptizing" another.[8] Moreover, "while most cleansing rites were repeated as often as one became unclean"—we might think of Jesus's washing of his disciples' feet in John 13—"the ordination washing was once-for-all."[9] Thus, for those familiar with the priestly ordination, where one son of Aaron washed another to inaugurate his priestly service, we can see how John's baptism of Jesus presented Jesus in priestly fashion. As Nicholas Perrin puts it in his book *Jesus the Priest*, the Gospels "depict the baptism as an inaugural moment that marks off a priestly career."[10]

Fourth, Luke highlights Jesus's priesthood in his genealogy and his likeness to Adam. After Jesus's baptism, Luke traces Jesus's family history back to Adam—and from Adam to God. Luke writes, "Jesus, the son (as was supposed) of Joseph . . . the son of David, . . . the son of Abraham, . . . the son of Adam, the son of God" (3:23–38). As God's Son incarnate, Jesus is presented as a new and better Adam. However, by connecting Jesus to Adam, Luke explains in what manner we might think of Christ's priesthood—Jesus is not a son of Levi but a son of God.[11] Admittedly, modern Christians might not make

---

7. Robert L. Webb, "Jesus' Baptism: Its Historicity and Implications," *Bulletin for Biblical Research* 10, no. 2 (2000): 280.

8. Leithart, *The Priesthood of the Plebs*, 95; Hank Voss, *The Priesthood of All Believers and the* Missio Dei: *A Canonical, Catholic, and Contextual Perspective*, Princeton Theological Monograph Series (Eugene, OR: Pickwick, 2016), 74–75.

9. Leithart, *The Priesthood of the Plebs*, 95.

10. Nicholas Perrin, *Jesus the Priest* (New York: SPCK, 2018), 88. In context, he is describing Matthew, Mark, and Luke.

11. On "son of God" as a priestly title, see Perrin, *Jesus the Priest*, 85; Leithart, *The Priesthood of the Plebs*, 118.

the priestly connection between Jesus and Adam, but based on the priestly vocation of Adam (detailed in chap. 1), we have reason for seeing this genealogy as furthering Luke's introduction to Jesus as a royal priest.

Luke's priestly focus is also observed in Jesus's age. Luke 3:23 notes that Jesus is "about thirty," the same age that priests began their ministry.[12] In this reference, Luke adds a minor detail to highlight Jesus's priestly service. Going further, Jesus's priesthood is immediately tested, as the Spirit of God takes him into the wilderness to be tempted by Satan. In Genesis, Adam failed to remove the unclean serpent from God's garden-temple but instead violated God's covenant with him. By contrast, Jesus succeeds in repelling the lies of Satan. He proves his priestly faithfulness by clinging to God's word and refusing to grasp for bread, glory, or power. This temptation narrative promises that Jesus will succeed where all priests, going back to Adam, failed.

Fifth, Jesus's arrival promises to fulfill the words of the prophets. In addition to standing in contrast to the priests who failed in the Old Testament, Jesus is presented as the fulfillment of Zechariah's promise of a royal priest. In a book that focuses on God's temple (e.g., John 1:14, 51; 2:18–22; 4:20–24) and Christ's sacrifice (e.g., John 1:29; 10:11; 11:49–53; 15:14), it is fitting that John also addresses Christ's priesthood.[13] And in Jesus's encounter with Nathanael, we find a priestly introduction to Jesus.

John 1:43–51 records the scene. When Philip invites Nathanael to meet Jesus, Nathanael infamously doubts whether anything good

---

12. See Num. 4:3, 23, 30, 35, 39–40, 43, 47; 1 Chron. 23:3. Likewise, the repetition of Levi's name in Luke 3:24, 29, and in v. 32 the mention of David's son Nathan, whose son Zabud is identified as a priest in 1 Kings 4:5, stress the point that Luke is doing all he can to connect Jesus with the priesthood. Leithart, *The Priesthood of the Plebs*, 117.

13. On the themes of temple and sacrifice, see Paul M. Hoskins, *Jesus as the Fulfillment of the Temple in the Gospel of John*, Paternoster Biblical Monographs (Eugene, OR: Wipf & Stock, 2006).

can come from Nazareth (v. 46). His mind changes, however, when Jesus says to him, "Before Philip called you, when you were under the fig tree, I saw you" (v. 48). To this otherwise unimpressive statement, Nathanael exclaims: "Rabbi, you are the Son of God! You are the King of Israel!" (v. 49). What could cause such a drastic change in Nathanael? Zechariah 3 seems to be the best answer.

In that passage, Zechariah promised the purification of the priesthood (vv. 1–5), the coming of "the Branch" (v. 8), and the restoration of the kingdom described in the language of vine and fig trees: "In that day, declares the LORD of hosts, every one of you will *invite his neighbor* to come under his vine and under his *fig tree*" (v. 10). Going back to the days of Solomon, sitting under one's own fig tree was a symbol of a flourishing kingdom (1 Kings 4:25).[14] From this mention of the fig tree coupled with the language of invitation (italicized above), we see how Philip's invitation of Nathanael fulfills Zechariah 3, a passage that promises a new royal priest.

More exactly, when Jesus identifies Nathanael as a true Israelite sitting under his fig tree (John 1:48), John is showing how Jesus fulfills the Law and the Prophets (1:45)—meaning that Jesus is the greater Joshua who will bring salvation to his people.[15] In other words, as someone looking for the kingdom of God, Nathanael recognizes who is addressing him. Jesus is the true priest of Zechariah 3. Just as John identified Jesus as the true temple (1:14) and true sacrifice (1:29) in the opening chapter of his Gospel, he also introduces Jesus as true priest.

In sum, the Gospels go to great lengths to introduce Jesus. Here we have seen the way Luke and John identify Jesus's priesthood.[16]

---

14. Jesus makes use of this imagery again at the Lord's Supper (see Matt. 26:29; Mark 14:25; Luke 22:18).

15. It is important to remember that "Jesus" and "Joshua" both translate the same Greek name.

16. For another introduction to Jesus and his priesthood from the Gospel of Mark, see Crispin H. T. Fletcher-Louis, "Jesus as the High Priestly Messiah: Part 2," *Journal for the Study of the Historical Jesus* 5 (2007): 57–79.

Now we will begin to see that reality unfold in the rest of his life, as he begins to carry out his priestly actions.

Jesus Acts like a Priest

If the Gospels made only passing comments to Jesus's priesthood in their opening chapters, we may not have confidence that Jesus is a priest in the Gospels. Yet, when we look at these four books, we see Jesus doing what priests do throughout. He teaches the law, purifies the unclean, cleanses the temple, forgives sins, and prays for his disciples. His actions also include the sacrifice he offers to God, but we will consider that in the next section. For now, we will see how these five activities form a priestly composite of Christ in the Gospels.

First, Jesus's teaching points to his priesthood. For instance, Jesus's gospel *of the kingdom* is a message with a *priestly* center. Instead of bringing a message of political change, Jesus pronounces forgiveness of sins (Matt. 9:2; cf. Lev. 4:20, 26, 31, 35; 5:10; etc.). Likewise, his ministry of teaching (Matt. 4:23–25; 9:35) reflects what priests did (Lev. 10:11; Deut. 17:9–11; 33:10; Mal. 2:6–7). Levitical priests separated the clean from the unclean; so too Jesus's teaching separates those purified by faith from those defiled by unbelief (Matt. 15).[17] As Nicholas Perrin puts it, "The making of ritual pronouncements of clean and unclean, holy and profane, was fundamentally . . . a *priestly activity.*"[18] In fact, we will even see this taking place on the cross, as Jesus hangs between two thieves—one who believes, one who does not.

Getting into specifics, Jesus begins with eight beatitudes in his Sermon on the Mount (Matt. 5:3–10). These words of blessing recall

---

17. Matthew 15 contains a debate with the Pharisees and the scribes about what makes someone clean. Jesus shows how priestly traditions have polluted the law (vv. 1–9) and how faith purifies the heart (vv. 10–28).

18. Perrin, *Jesus the Priest*, 111 (emphasis his).

the type of priestly benediction Aaron would give to Israel (see Num. 6:24–26). More precisely, the first four beatitudes (Matt. 5:3–6) contain literary connections to Isaiah 61, a passage that promises a new priesthood (Isa. 61:5–6). Next, Jesus calls his disciples "the salt of the earth" (Matt. 5:13). This peculiar description harkens back to the covenant of salt made with Levi (Num. 18:19; cf. Lev. 2:13; 2 Chron. 13:5).[19] And in the Lord's Prayer, which invites Jesus's disciples to address God as "Father," we find the petition, "Give us today our daily bread" (Matt. 6:9, 11). Both the prayer and the provision of daily bread are suggestive of the priesthood (Lev. 24:5–9).[20] All in all, when considering Jesus's ministry of the word, we should remember the role priests played in teaching, because in Jesus's teaching we discover that he is more than a prophet; he is also a priest.[21]

Luke also highlights the teaching ministry of Jesus. When Jesus returns to Galilee from his temptation in the desert, he enters the synagogue on the Sabbath and reads from Isaiah 61:1–2:

> The Spirit of the Lord is upon me,
>> because he has anointed me
>> to proclaim good news to the poor.
> He has sent me to proclaim release to the captives
>> and recovery of sight to the blind,
>> to set at liberty those who are oppressed,
> to proclaim the year of the Lord's favor. (Luke 4:17–19)

Jesus then offers these shocking words: "Today this Scripture has been fulfilled in your hearing" (Luke 4:21). As we saw in chapter 3, Isaiah 61 is loaded with priestly imagery. Just a few verses earlier, Isaiah

---

19. Perrin, *Jesus the Priest*, 112–28.

20. These observations only scratch the surface of all the priestly elements of the Lord's Prayer. Perrin, *Jesus the Priest*, 17–53.

21. It may help to know that when Jesus is presented as a prophet, he is a prophet like Moses, who was both a prophet and a priest.

spoke of the Redeemer coming to Zion to bring salvation (59:20), and this divine warrior is clad in priestly attire (59:17). Similarly, just a few verses after the text that Jesus quotes, Isaiah 61:5–6 reads,

> Strangers shall stand and tend your flocks;
>> foreigners shall be your plowmen and vinedressers;
> but you shall be called the priests of the LORD;
>> they shall speak of you as the ministers of our God.

By stating that this passage has been fulfilled in their hearing, Jesus reveals how Isaiah's new covenant promises are coming true. In Christ, we find a Spirit-anointed servant whose atonement for sin will produce sons and daughters that are simultaneously fellow priests. This is the vision of Isaiah, and when we read Jesus's words and his ensuing calls for discipleship in light of Isaiah, we can see how the disciples are more than religious followers—they are a family of priests brought into the kingdom by the priestly ministry of Christ's word.[22]

Second, Jesus's ministry of healing is a priestly activity. Going beyond teaching, Matthew 8:1–4 recounts the time Jesus heals a leper. Placing this after the Sermon on the Mount, Matthew continues his focus on his priestly role.[23] In Leviticus 13–14, God assigned priests to render a verdict on leprosy. Now something similar occurs in Matthew 8. Instead of issuing a judgment, however, Jesus puts his hands on the leper and makes him clean. Whereas lepers would defile anyone they touched under the old covenant—including priests—here Jesus, as the harbinger of the new covenant, communicates his cleanness to this man through physical touch.

---

22. John 6:45 is another place where Jesus's ministry of teaching surfaces. Citing Isa. 54:13, it reads, "And they will all be taught by God." This promise highlights the greater efficacy of the new covenant that Jesus will bring (cf. Jer. 31:31–34)—a new covenant inaugurated by his priestly sacrifice and his priestly ministry of teaching.

23. As Matt. 4:23–25 and 9:35 bookend Matt. 5–9 with summaries of Christ's teaching and healing, these intermediate chapters illustrate how his teaching and healing stand together.

After Jesus's heals this leper, he sends him to the priests. But why—what is the message Jesus wants this cleansed leper to bring to the priests? Namely, that a new priest is in town and he has the power to make lepers clean.[24] Just as Ezekiel 44:19 promised, Jesus's healing brings holiness.[25] In this way, healing is a glimpse of the new creation and an indication that Jesus's offer of forgiveness is accompanied by power to heal, or even raise the dead (Matt. 9:18–26).

Third, Jesus is able to purify the temple. As we saw in 1–2 Chronicles, priests sanctified the Holy Place of God. After unrighteous kings brought idols into the temple, righteous kings employed the priests to purify God's house so that God's people could worship again. Strikingly, Jesus does the same when he drives out the money changers in Matthew 21:12–17, only he does not outsource the purification to someone else. Rather, picking up words from Isaiah 56:7, Jesus says, "It is written, 'My house shall be called a house of prayer,' but you make it a den of robbers" (Matt. 21:13). In his enacted parable, Jesus declares the temple unclean, even as he drives out those defiling its precincts. In this cleansing, Jesus acts like a priest purifying God's house.

Fourth, Jesus's authority to forgive sin demonstrates his priesthood. In Mark 2 Jesus forgives a paralytic, inciting the scribes to ask, "Who can forgive sins but God alone?" (v. 7). Proving his authority to forgive sin, Jesus replies, "'That you may know that the Son of Man has authority on earth to forgive sins'—he said to the paralytic—'I say to

---

24. Nicholas G. Piotrowski and David S. Schrock, "'You Can Make Me Clean': The Matthean Jesus as Priest and the Biblical-Theological Results," *Criswell Theological Review* 14, no. 1 (2016): 3–14.

25. Observe the way Matt. 9:20–22 shines a light on Christ's (priestly?) garment when the bleeding woman touches the fringe of his robe (cf. Num. 15:37–38). Leviticus 15:19 declares a bleeding woman unclean, but by her contact with Christ's clothing she is healed. In contrast to the priests' fringes, made long to make others think highly of them (Matt. 23:5), Jesus's fringes bring healing to bless others (Matt. 14:35), just as Ezekiel promised (42:14; 44:19).

you, rise, pick up your bed, and go home'" (vv. 10–11). Clearly, this passage identifies the divinity of Christ. God alone can forgive sins, and his pronouncement of forgiveness vividly affirms this truth.

At the same time, Jesus's pronouncement of forgiveness is also priestly. In Israel, God pronounced forgiveness *through the priests* (cf. Lev. 4:20, 26, 31, 35; 5:10; etc.).[26] And here Jesus is shown to possess an authority superseding the priests—he is able to forgive *and* heal. While the Levitical priests granted forgiveness, they could not grant life. According to Leviticus 21:14–24, priests could only exclude the crippled; they could not bring them into God's holy spaces. Yet Jesus enables the forgiven man to rise, pick up his bed, go to his house, and then reenter covenant life in Israel. Importantly, this episode demonstrates how Christ's authority to forgive is a shared property of his two natures—as God the Son, Jesus has authority to grant forgiveness by nature of his divinity and by nature of his priestly vocation.

Fifth, Jesus prays for his people. Though prayer alone does not make Jesus a priest, it is one of the aspects of his priesthood. Throughout his life Jesus is observed praying.[27] When he selects his twelve disciples, he prays (Luke 6:12–16); when he reveals his identity to Peter and the disciples, he prays (Luke 9:18–20); when he reveals the glory of his kingdom, it is in the context of prayer (Luke 9:28–36); and in the hours leading up to his arrest, he prays fervently in the garden of Gethsemane (Matt. 26:36–46).

In particular, we find Jesus praying for his people according to their needs. For instance, he prays for Peter, to protect him from Satan when the evil one seeks to sift Peter like wheat (Luke 22:31–32). Like-

---

26. In Israel, God grants forgiveness through the cultic system of worship. Forgiveness is procured by a sacrifice for sin, it is granted at the temple, and it is pronounced by a priest. In this instance, Jesus's pronouncement of forgiveness outside the temple violates the strictures of the law and invites the anger of the scribes. This reading of Mark 2 doesn't deny Jesus's deity; it explains how the God-man grants forgiveness.

27. Examples of Jesus praying can be found in Matt. 14:23; 19:13; 26:36–46; Mark 1:35.

wise, Jesus intercedes for those who put him to death (Luke 23:34).[28] And most marvelously, we find Jesus's "high priestly prayer" in John 17. In this elongated prayer, Jesus prays for his disciples and for those who will believe their message (v. 20). Like the priests of Israel, who brought the names of the people into the Holy Place by means of their priestly attire (Ex. 28:29), so Jesus prays for his own—those whom the Father has given him from out of the world (John 17:6).[29] And he prays for their endurance and sanctification (vv. 15, 17).

Finally, Jesus's priestly ministry of prayer is seen when he raises his hands like the high priest of old to bless his people in Luke 24:50. Granted, this prayer occurs after his death and resurrection, but the point remains—Jesus blesses his people like a priest.

In sum, these five actions—(1) teaching the law, (2) purifying the unclean, (3) cleansing the temple, (4) forgiving sins, and (5) praying for his own—demonstrate Jesus's priestly vocation. Again, in these actions Jesus is not called a priest, nor does he assign himself that title. Yet, for those who know what priests do, his actions are unmistakable. In his earthly life, Jesus acts like a priest, and now as we turn to his cross, we will see Jesus in his most priestly action yet—the offering of himself as a sacrifice for sin.

Jesus Makes an Efficacious Sacrifice

The great Puritan John Owen once defined priesthood by the singular role of sacrifice.[30] As we have seen in this book, priesthood

---

28. On the efficacy of this prayer, see Stephen J. Wellum, "The New Covenant Work of Christ: Priesthood, Atonement, and Intercession," in *From Heaven He Came and Sought Her: Definite Atonement in Historical, Biblical, Theological, and Pastoral Perspective*, ed. David Gibson and Jonathan Gibson (Wheaton, IL: Crossway, 2013), 531–32.

29. Put negatively, Jesus does not pray for the world in general (John 17:9), because the world (i.e., all the people of the world) has not been given to him. He prays for those people whom the Father gave him before the foundation of the world.

30. In his classic treatment on Christ's priesthood, John Owen called the priest a "sacrificer." Owen, *The Priesthood of Christ: Its Necessity and Nature* (Fearn, Ross-shire, Scotland: Christian Heritage, 2010), 38.

entails more than sacrifice, but in a world corrupted by sin, it cannot mean less. Attempts to deny Christ's priestly sacrifice fail because at the heart of his ministry is the sacrifice Jesus offers on the cross.[31] In each Gospel we can see how Jesus moves toward the cross, which is the pinnacle of his priestly work.

Matthew. Citing Psalm 110 twice in the final week of his life, Jesus identifies himself with this royal priestly psalm as he prepares to go to the cross. First, after a long debate with the scribes and Pharisees about who has authority in the temple (Matt. 21:23–22:46), Jesus quotes Psalm 110, asking whom David is describing (Matt. 22:41–46). Clearly, Jesus sees himself as David's Lord, the priest like Melchizedek described in David's psalm.

Second, as the high priest interrogates Jesus (Matt. 26:61–63), Jesus replies, "But I tell you, from now on you will see the Son of Man seated at the right hand of Power and coming on the clouds of heaven" (v. 64).[32] Jesus lets Scripture—in this case, Psalm 110 and Daniel 7—bear witness to him, and the point is unmistakable: Jesus *is* the long-awaited royal priest, the one whose sacrifice will bring righteousness and peace. In response, the high priest condemns Jesus (Matt. 26:65–68), proving the former has no business standing before God.[33] Simultaneously, Jesus proves he is the royal priest by his absolute trust in God's word. Proceeding to the cross, Jesus offers himself as a sacrifice for the sins of others.

---

31. This is the errant conclusion of Richard Nelson, *Raising Up a Faithful Priest: Community and Priesthood in Biblical Theology* (Louisville: Westminster John Knox, 1993), who denies penal substitution. Such a denial will not work, for the sacrificial system demanded priests to offer sacrifices to expiate sin and propitiate the wrath of God.

32. In general, any time apostles refer to the "right hand" of God (e.g., Acts 2:33; 5:31; 7:55) they are applying Ps. 110 to Christ and his church.

33. It is striking that the priest tears his robe, just as the temple veil will be torn in Christ's crucifixion. While the words for "tear" and "torn" are different (cf. Matt. 26:65 and 27:51), the connection should not be missed. As Ex. 25–27 clothes the high priest in robes made of the same material as the tabernacle, so here the end of the priesthood and the end of the temple are concurrent.

Matthew 20:28 prepares the reader for understanding the cross in this way, as does the priestly opposition to Jesus. In Matthew 21–28 we find a priestly competition between Jesus and the priests. Jesus's death tears the temple veil *and* opens a way for people to approach God (Matt. 27:51; cf. Heb. 10:19–24). This is seen in the events of the cross, which Jesus interprets to his disciples in the Lord's Supper (Matt. 26:26–29). The Supper, too, evidences the priesthood of Christ as it signifies that his death grants forgiveness (v. 28) and inaugurates a new covenant (cf. Luke 22:20). We will consider the Lord's Supper further when we get to Luke's Gospel.

Mark. In Mark's Gospel, Jesus speaks of "the Son of Man" each time he describes his coming death.[34] For those with ears to hear, "Son of Man" recalls Daniel 7:13–14, which begins to prepare us for seeing his cross as a place of humiliation, followed by exaltation. Importantly, Daniel 7:13–14 supplies this pattern too. In verse 14, the Son of Man is given rule and authority over all the earth, indicating the dominion he will have. This dominion, however, comes after he has "come on the clouds"—that is, when he is "presented" or brought near to God in verse 13. This language of "clouds" and "coming near" recaptures the high priest's approach to God on the Day of Atonement (Lev. 16:1–13).[35] Indeed, as royal and priestly themes often overlap in Scripture, Daniel 7:13–14 is no different. The royal inheritance that Jesus will receive is due to the priestly service he will perform. Thus, when Jesus uses Daniel's terminology to speak of his cross, it is important to see how this ancient text informs the meaning of his death. Getting specific, Mark gives two ways in which Daniel 7 helps explain that Jesus's death is a priestly offering.

---

34. Mark 8:31–33; 9:30–32; 10:32–34; cf. 8:38; 9:9, 12; 14:21, 41.
35. See the discussion of "clouds" and "coming near" in Perrin, *Jesus the Priest*, 176–78.

First, in Mark 10:42–45 Jesus combines the language of Daniel 7 and Isaiah 53 to correct his power-hungry disciples (Mark 10:35–41). When he proclaims a gospel of the kingdom, Jesus's disciples understand his rule as purely political. They have not yet grasped the priestly nature of his kingdom. Hence, they fight for the right to sit in glory with him. In response, Jesus unites his kingdom to his suffering and explains that his kingdom is a priestly kingdom. He says, "For even the Son of Man came not to be served but to serve, and to give his life as a ransom for many" (Mark 10:45). Jesus did not come to be served, as wicked rulers do; he came to serve others and to die for the sins of his people. Applying Daniel 7 ("son of man") and Isaiah 53 ("ransom for many") to himself, Jesus says his death will fulfill the servant's priestly sacrifice. To put this doctrinally, Jesus's passive obedience is not, strictly speaking, passive.[36] Jesus is not only a willing sacrifice on the cross; he is an active priest.

Second, Mark 13 uses imagery from Daniel 7 to explain Christ's sacrifice. While many read Mark 13 as a prediction of future events, I am convinced we should read it as an apocalyptic explanation of Christ's impending sacrifice.[37] On this reading, Mark 13:24–26 describes not Jesus's second coming but his immediate death, resurrection, and ascension. As verse 26 describes "the Son of Man coming in clouds," it picks up Daniel 7:13 and applies it to Jesus. As we saw in chapter 4, Daniel takes up the language of Leviticus 16:13 ("the cloud of incense" covering the "mercy seat") to explain the work of the Son of Man. Nicholas Perrin concludes:

---

36. Few articulate the beauty of "Christ's priestly action in his death" like Hugh Martin, *The Atonement: In Its Relations to the Covenant, the Priesthood, the Intercession of Our Lord* (London: Nisbet, 1870), 69–95.

37. The following reading of Mark has been largely informed by Peter G. Bolt, *The Cross from a Distance: Atonement in Mark's Gospel*, New Studies in Biblical Theology (Downers Grove, IL: InterVarsity Press, 2005), esp. 85–115; Bolt, "Mark 13: An Apocalyptic Precursor to the Passion Narrative," *Reformed Theological Review* 54, no. 1 (1995): 10–32.

By promising his confronters that they would see him "seated at the right hand" and "coming on the clouds," activities reserved for the Melchizedekian high priest (Psalm 110) and the [Day of Atonement]-officiating Son of Man (Daniel 7), respectively, . . . Jesus affirms that they would see him providing atonement for God's people. . . . *He would die, in other words, as the true priest.*[38]

In this reading, Mark uses Day of Atonement imagery from Daniel 7:13 to give a theological explanation for Christ's once-and-for-all purification of God's house. In Mark, this will mean judgment for Jerusalem's temple, even as it inaugurates a new covenant (14:22–25) and forms a new temple. To put it differently, and to pick up on Psalm 118, the stone rejected by the builders will become the cornerstone (Mark 12:10–11; cf. Ps. 118:22–23). In this way, "The goal of redemptive-history, that God would dwell with his people, is accomplished through the atoning and temple-building work of the (priestly) Son of David."[39]

In sum, Christ's priestly sacrifice illumines the priestly showdown in Mark 14:53–64. Arrested and brought before the grand inquisitor, Jesus is questioned on who he is and what he has taught. In response, Jesus conjoins again the words of Daniel 7 and Psalm 110: "Again the high priest asked him, 'Are you the Christ, the Son of the Blessed?' And Jesus said, 'I am, and you will see the Son of Man seated at the right hand of Power, and coming with the clouds of heaven'" (Mark 14:61–62). In his life Jesus's royal priesthood was not recognized. Ironically, many do not recognize his priesthood in the Gospels either. Yet, from a close reading of Mark, we learn how Christ's sacrifice reveals his royal priesthood.

---

38. Perrin, *Jesus the Priest*, 279 (emphasis mine).
39. Nicholas Piotrowski, "'Whatever You Ask' for the Missionary Purposes of the Eschatological Temple: Quotation and Typology in Mark 11–12," *Southern Baptist Journal of Theology* 21, no. 1 (2017): 112.

Luke. If Luke takes such effort to introduce Jesus in priestly terms,[40] then it should not surprise us that when he speaks of Christ's cross, he also employs priestly imagery. On the cross, Jesus prays for his persecutors (23:34), promises the repentant thief a place in paradise (23:43), and entrusts himself to the Father after the temple veil is torn (23:45–46). In these words from the cross, Jesus continues to do what priests do—he prays, he distinguishes between people, and he approaches the throne of God, even making a way for believers to come to God. Still, it is in the Lord's Supper, initiated on the night before his crucifixion, that we find the clearest evidence for his priestly sacrifice.

The Lord's Supper reflects Christ's priesthood in at least three ways. First, in celebrating the Passover, we are brought to the festival that recalls the time when God had all fathers in Israel serve as priests by applying blood to their doorposts, thus delivering their firstborn sons from death. Now, as the host of this Passover meal, Jesus assumes a priestly role as he leads his people to remember his death. Second, the mention of a "new covenant" is unique to Luke—Matthew and Mark do not speak of a "new covenant." Such use of this term (previously found only in Jer. 31:31) suggests that Luke is presenting Jesus's meal in light of what Jeremiah said—namely, that a royal figure will draw near to God (Jer. 30:21) in order to establish a new covenant. Third, the use of bread and wine, common elements in covenant ceremonies, harkens back to the priestly meal Melchizedek shared with Abraham (Gen. 14:18).[41] The connection is subtle, but held in Jerusalem, the city of Melchizedek, where Abraham (Genesis 22) and David offered sacrifices (2 Samuel 24), this first Lord's Supper prepares Jesus's disciples for his own sacrifice. In

---

40. See above (p. 121), "Jesus's Birth and Baptism Introduce Us to Jesus the Priest."
41. John H. Sailhamer, *The Pentateuch as Narrative: A Biblical-Theological Commentary* (Grand Rapids, MI: Zondervan, 1995), 147.

the cross, we come to the reality to which all the previous priestly sacrifices point.

In all, Jesus is the Passover Lamb who will be slain to save his people, but he is also the faithful priest who offers himself as the true sacrifice. Indeed, Jesus's words on the cross confirm his priestly status. He is not only a lamb silently led to the slaughter (cf. Isa. 53:7); he is also a priest speaking the words of God from the altar (Isa. 50:4). Read in tandem, the Lord's Supper and Christ's crucifixion help us to see how Jesus offers himself on the cross, just as a priest would bring the blood near to God to atone for his people's sin.

John. John's Gospel also portrays Christ's priesthood in relationship to the cross. First, in John 10:11 Jesus speaks of the way he will lay down his life for the sheep like a good shepherd. Soon thereafter, in verses 17–18, he speaks of his proactive will and divine power to lay down his life: "For this reason the Father loves me, because I lay down my life that I may take it up again. No one takes it from me, but I lay it down of my own accord. I have authority to lay it down, and I have authority to take it up again. This charge I have received from my Father." And then, in the next chapter, John includes the words of Caiaphas the high priest, who prophesies that Jesus's death will save the nation and the world (11:51–53).

Though these verses do not call Jesus a priest, they do demonstrate his proactive participation in offering up his life. As Hugh Martin has described the cross, it is Jesus's "altar of priestly agency."[42] His death is something that he does, not just something done to him. And thus in John's Gospel, which spends so much time developing the obedience of the Son, we see the greatest obedience in his priestly sacrifice. As he says in his priestly prayer, "For their sake I consecrate myself, that they also may be sanctified in truth" (John 17:19). Jesus's

---

42. Martin, *The Atonement*, 74.

act of consecration is his self-offering on the cross. This is his priestly sacrifice, which effectively redeems the people whom the Father gave him before the world began.

A Priestly King

The Gospels never call Jesus a "priest," but as Jesus said, "Each tree is known by its own fruit" (Luke 6:44). In this case, a priest is known by his actions. Because true priesthood "is primarily about *doing* things, . . . rather than about *being* a particular kind of person or having a particular genealogical descent,"[43] we can say with confidence that the Gospels present Jesus as a royal priest.

Born as a son of David, Jesus proves himself to be a priestly type of king. Even though he never asserts his priesthood, his life towers over the Levitical priests. As I have defined priesthood from the Old Testament, we see in Jesus the perfect embodiment of holy service. Indeed, all four Gospels present him as serving his heavenly Father by means of sanctifying God's place, sacrificing himself for God's people, and speaking God's word. Truly, in the face of false priests and unbelieving Levites, Jesus is best understood as a true priest to whom the Levitical priesthood is but a fleeting shadow. Now we only need to see how his priesthood is shared with his new covenant people. This is what we will consider next.

---

43. Deborah W. Rooke, "Kingship as Priesthood: The Relationship between the High Priesthood and the Monarchy," in *King and Messiah in Israel and the Ancient Near East*, ed. John Day, Journal for the Study of the Old Testament Supplement Series 270 (Sheffield, England: Sheffield Academic, 1998), 189 (emphasis hers).

6

Acts through Revelation

The Royal Priesthood Multiplies

If you have read this book from the beginning, you will be familiar with the royal priesthood—patterned in creation, legislated in the Law, compromised and promised in the Prophets, and anticipated in the Writings. Moving into the New Testament, we saw how the long-expected royal priest arrived in Jesus Christ. Now—from Acts to Revelation—we will see what Christ's priesthood means for his people and how his people (especially the author of Hebrews) understand the meaning of his priesthood.

In this concluding chapter, therefore, we will see what Scripture says about Christ's high priesthood and how Christ makes his church a kingdom of priests. In particular, we will look at Acts, the letters of Paul and Peter, Hebrews, and Revelation to see how Christ's royal priesthood multiplies in the church and what it means for us today.[1]

---

1. This chapter will be selective in its consideration of Paul and the General Epistles.

The Priesthood Inaugurated in Acts

If Luke began his Gospel by drawing attention to Christ's priesthood, it appears he has done the same with Acts. It begins, "In the first book, O Theophilus, I have dealt with all that Jesus *began* to do and teach" (1:1). The implication is that the resurrected Christ continues to minister by his word and his Spirit. As he sits enthroned in heaven, he is simultaneously present on earth with his people (cf. Matt. 28:18–20; Acts 9:4–6; Eph. 2:17; Rev. 1:13, 20).

Proving this point, Luke records Jesus's ascension in Acts 1:1–11. Rather than calling Jesus a priest, he reports the very moment when the Father honors Christ with the priestly throne promised in Psalm 110. In Acts 1:9–11 Jesus ascends to heaven, where he is seated at God's right hand (see Acts 2:33; 5:31; 7:55–56). In other words, Luke begins Acts by showing how Jesus is the priest-king seated in glory. This immediate application of Psalm 110 is important because it gives context for the arrival of the Spirit in Acts 2.

At Pentecost, we see how Spirit-baptism consecrates the church for service. Just as Jesus's baptism ordained him for priestly service, now his greater baptism—the baptism in the Spirit—identifies and empowers the people who will serve as priests in his kingdom. Pentecost is what marks out Christ's royal priests. Just as Aaron's ministry was bolstered by the addition of Levites (Num. 3:11–13; 8:14–16; 18:7), so Christ receives from the Father priests made clean by the Spirit.

Admittedly, this priestly reading requires a good bit of Old Testament background. But that is the kind of biblical theology we find in Acts. In fact, we find at least three priestly elements in Acts. These aspects of priesthood correspond to the definition of priesthood we have followed through the book—namely, that priests stand to serve God by sanctifying a place, offering a sacrifice, and speaking God's covenant word. These priestly actions are no longer restricted to the priests and Levites; they are true for all who have been baptized in the Spirit.

First, the church becomes the place of holy worship where priests serve in God's presence. In the Old Testament, priests served at altars from Bethel to Sinai to Jerusalem, but now worship will occur wherever the Spirit gathers God's saints. While the church in Jerusalem gathers in the temple for a time (Acts 2:46; 5:42), it will spread quickly to the ends of the earth. Acts tells the story of how Christ pours out the Spirit on all flesh (i.e., Jew and Gentile) and brings worship from Jerusalem to Rome and everywhere in between. As Paul will later refer to the church as the "temple" of the living God (1 Cor. 3:16–17; 6:19; 2 Cor. 6:16; Eph. 2:21), and Peter, the "spiritual house" of God made of living stones (1 Pet. 2:5), Acts shows the Spirit assembling God's people into local temples of Christian worship.

Though the language of priests is not attributed to these disciples, Acts 2:42 describes the activities of the church in ways that reflect priestly worship: "And they devoted themselves to the apostles' teaching and the fellowship, to the breaking of bread and the prayers." Incredibly, each of these elements of worship continues practices from the temple. Instead of listening to the priests teach the law, Christ's disciples listen to the apostles, who replace the priests. Instead of offering sacrifices at Jerusalem's temple, now church members share their gifts with one another (Acts 2:44–45). Instead of eating the sacrifices associated with Israel's festivals, now they break bread and remember the Lord's sacrifice in his new covenant meal. Moreover, the disciples of Christ offer prayer to God through Christ (cf. Acts 4:23–31). No longer are their prayers directed to the temple (cf. 1 Kings 8:29–30, 35, 38, 42); now they lift their voices to the God of heaven (Acts 4:24) through Jesus Christ, the high priest seated in glory. In all these ways, the establishment of a new temple—comprising myriad local assemblies—demonstrates how the church is the place where God's priests are found.

Second, Acts shows how priests and Levites are added to the church. While the main focus of Acts demonstrates the positive work of the Spirit, there are hints that the old covenant is coming to an end. One example of this is the ministry of Barnabas. Acts 4:36–37 introduces him as a son of Levi who sells a piece of land and lays the proceeds at the apostles' feet. This act not only models the way God is going to provide for the church (4:32–37) but also reveals how this Levite turns from the old covenant to the new. Though Luke never explains the meaning of this sale, the mention of Barnabas's Levitical heritage is not accidental. Barnabas is an example of someone turning from his heritage in the law to his inheritance in Christ.

Another place where Luke highlights the end of the old covenant is in the conversion of priests in Acts 6. Verse 7 says, "The word of God continued to increase, and the number of the disciples multiplied greatly in Jerusalem, and a great many of the priests became obedient to the faith." This offhand comment is remarkable. It shows that some who opposed Jesus in his life were now coming to faith. Moreover, this verse sets up the ministry of Stephen, who both speaks against the temple and confounds the Jews. Luke places Saul in the context of Stephen's ministry with significant clues suggesting that Stephen's preaching and praying ("Lord, do not hold this sin against them"—Acts 7:60) prepares the way for Saul's conversion.

This is the third instance of a Jewish leader surrendering to Christ. As Paul identifies himself in Philippians 3:5, he is "of the tribe of Benjamin, a Hebrew of Hebrews; . . . [and] a Pharisee." In his pedigree, he does not identify himself as a priest. Yet, as he dedicates his life to protecting the law, he persecutes the church to protect all of the institutions established by Moses, the Levitical priesthood included. When Christ confronts him on the road to Damascus, however, he believes the gospel, which includes a belief that Jesus is the true royal priest. In his conversion, Paul becomes the chief evangelist to the Gentiles. Romans explains that he sees his ministry to the Gentiles as a priestly endeavor (15:16), but before we turn there, we need to make one more observation in Acts.

Third, Gentiles receiving the Spirit is a sign that the kingdom of priests has come. In places like Isaiah 66:19–21, God promised that in the last days Gentiles would furnish the kingdom with priests and Levites. In Acts this begins to happen in real time. As the Ethiopian eunuch (8:26–38), God-fearers from Cornelius's house (10:44–48), and Gentiles from Ephesus (19:1–7) receive the Spirit, Luke shows how God is making priests from all the nations. Each of these brings fulfillment to the Prophets (cf. Isa. 56:3–5; Joel 2:28–32; Mal. 3:1–4) and confirms that the one reigning in heaven is bringing his kingdom to the earth through the witness of his church. To be clear, Acts does not make explicit connections between the priestly promises of the Old Testament and their fulfillment in Christ's church, but when we read Acts with the rest of the Bible, we can see how Acts reveals the origins of Christ's royal priesthood.

The Priesthood Expanded in Paul and Peter

In their book *Representing Christ: A Vision for the Priesthood of All Believers*, Uche Anizor and Hank Voss list seven practices of new covenant priests: (1) baptism, (2) prayer, (3) *lectio divina* (reading Scripture), (4) church discipline, (5) ministry to one another, (6) proclamation, and (7) the Lord's Supper.[2] These seven practices

---

2. Uche Anizor and Hank Voss, *Representing Christ: A Vision for the Priesthood of All Believers* (Downers Grove, IL: IVP Academic, 2016), 111–46.

compose the "spiritual sacrifices" that the church offers today as a kingdom of priests (see Rom. 12:1–2; 1 Pet. 2:5–10).

In our study, we have seen how many of these practices were carried out by the Levitical priests and repeated by Jesus. Now, as we enter the epistles of Paul and Peter, we will see how these inspired authors urge the church to carry out their priestly calling in Christ. Indeed, following our definition of the priesthood, we will look at how the church is called to (1) sanctify the house of God, (2) offer spiritual sacrifices, and (3) speak the words of God in prayer and evangelism.

The Church Sanctifies the House of God

In Paul's letters, we find regular use of cultic imagery. For example, Paul speaks of the church as a temple (1 Cor. 3:16–17; 6:19; 2 Cor. 6:14–7:1), ministry as a living sacrifice (Rom. 12:1), and evangelism as a "priestly service" (Rom. 15:16). Likewise, Peter applies the language of Exodus 19:6 ("royal priesthood") to the church, saying:

> You yourselves like living stones are being built up as a spiritual house, to be a holy priesthood, to offer spiritual sacrifices acceptable to God through Jesus Christ. . . .
>
> But you are a chosen race, a royal priesthood, a holy nation, a people for his own possession, that you may proclaim the excellencies of him who called you out of darkness into his marvelous light. (1 Pet. 2:5, 9)

Priestly imagery is not absent in these epistles. When we put all the data together, it is very present. Peter is most explicit in his use of Exodus, but Paul is equally concerned with describing the church as a priestly people. As Hank Voss notes, Paul's letters, "while containing unique melodies, harmonize around a common core of apostolic teaching [that concerns] an eschatologized temple, priesthood, and sacrifice."[3] In table 5, we can see how Paul speaks of these cultic elements as they are applied to Christ and the church throughout his letters.

Table 5. Paul's cultic language

	Christ	**The Church**
Temple	Temple (Col. 1:19; 2:9) Cornerstone (Eph. 2:20) Foundation (1 Cor. 3:11)	Temple (1 Cor. 3:16–17; 6:19; 2 Cor. 6:14–7:1; Eph. 2:18–22) God's house(hold) (Gal. 6:10; Eph. 2:19; 1 Tim. 3:15) Access (Rom. 5:2; Eph. 2:18; 3:12)
Sacrifice	Sacrifice (Eph. 5:1–2) Propitiation (Rom. 3:25) Blood (Rom. 5:9; 1 Cor. 11:25, 27; Eph. 1:7; 2:13; Col. 1:20)	Living sacrifice (Rom. 12:1–2) Fragrant offering (Phil. 4:18) Drink offering (Phil. 2:17; 2 Tim. 4:6) Offering (Rom. 15:16; Eph. 5:2)
Priest	Right hand of God (Rom. 8:34; Eph. 1:20; Col. 3:1) Intercession (Rom. 8:34) Mediator (1 Tim. 2:5; cf. Gal. 3:19–20)	Serve, worship (Rom. 1:9; 12:1; Phil. 3:3; 2 Tim. 1:3) Minister/ministry (Rom. 15:16; 2 Cor. 9:12; Phil. 2:17, 25, 30) Teach/teaching (Rom. 15:14; Col. 3:16; 1 Tim. 3:1–7; 2 Tim. 2:22–26; Titus 1:5–9)* Pray/prayer (Rom. 1:10; 10:1; 2 Cor. 1:11; 9:14; Eph. 6:18; Phil. 1:4, 9, 19; 4:6; Col. 1:3, 9; 4:3; 1 Thess. 5:17, 25; 2 Thess. 1:11; 3:1)

* The general ability to know God and exhort others in gospel truth (see, e.g., Rom. 15:14; Col. 3:16; cf. Acts 2:16–21) would include the gift of teachers to the church, hence the inclusion of the pastoral offices in this list. On the use of priestly language in the early church, see Cyril Eastwood, *The Royal Priesthood of the Faithful: An Investigation of the Doctrine from Biblical Times to the Reformation* (Minneapolis: Augsburg, 1963), 56–90.

From this survey of Paul's letters, we learn how Christians serve as priests in God's household. Just as the priests in Israel were brought near to God to serve in his temple and minister to God's people, now members of the church, which is the temple of the living God, are called to be priests to one another. Let's consider five ways the

3. Hank Voss, *The Priesthood of All Believers and the* Missio Dei: *A Canonical, Catholic, and Contextual Perspective*, Princeton Theological Monograph Series (Eugene, OR: Pickwick, 2016), 42. Voss lists six letters associated with Rome (Romans, Philippians, Ephesians, 2 Timothy, Hebrews, and 1 Peter) that all address priestly themes.

church, identified as a family of royal priests and empowered by the Holy Spirit, sanctifies the household of God.

First, the church is a people who have been raised to the right hand of God. In Ephesians 1:19–20 Paul prays for the believers to know their hope, their glorious inheritance, and God's power at work in them, which is the same "that he worked in Christ when he raised him from the dead and seated him at his right hand in the heavenly places." By citing Christ's position at God's right hand, Paul identifies Christ as the royal priest of Psalm 110. Then Ephesians 2:5 applies that psalm to the church: "God . . . made us alive together with Christ . . . and raised us up with him and *seated us with him in the heavenly places in Christ Jesus.*" Just as Psalm 110 images a union of the priest-king with his people, so Ephesians 2 assigns the covenantal blessing of Christ to his people. The significance of this is that just as priests served as priests in God's temple, so now the church does the same—as a people given access to the temple of God.

Second, the church is a people called to serve God in his temple. In Ephesians 2, Paul moves from seating Christians in "heavenly places" (v. 6) to the place where heaven touches earth—the temple (vv. 19–22). In a context where Christ reconciles Jew and Gentile as one new man (vv. 11–18), Paul describes the church as a temple composed of Spirit-filled saints. Mixing architectural and arboreal imagery, he paints the church as a new Eden, one where the members of God's household are servants together in the household of faith.

By attending to Paul's typology, we see how God gives his saints the priestly duty to serve one another as fellow saints (i.e., "holy ones") in the household of God. Indeed, Ephesians continues its focus on the temple through Ephesians 4, where members of Christ's body are given to the church as gifts to build up one another in love (vv. 1–16).

Importantly, Ephesians 4:8 cites Psalm 68:18, a passage with priestly connections to Numbers 8:9 and 18:6—two passages where Levites are "given" as gifts to the high priest.[4] From Paul's citation of Psalm 68, we learn how new covenant priests come to serve in God's new temple.[5] Ephesians 4:17–6:9 then goes on to explain how Spirit-filled believers are to conduct themselves as a kingdom of priests.

Third, the church participates in temple worship. Romans 12:1–2 is the classic text on this point, as it says that all who have received the mercies of God will offer themselves as living sacrifices. Romans 12–14 then explains how to serve one another in holiness. In Ephesians and Colossians, this household worship includes singing psalms, hymns, and spiritual songs (Eph. 5:18–20; Col. 3:16) and praying for God's word to succeed (Eph. 6:19; Col. 4:2–4). Moreover, Paul also speaks of giving to the work of the church in sacrificial terms. In Philippians he commends the church for their "fragrant offering" (4:18) after describing himself as being "poured out as a drink offering upon the sacrificial offering of your faith" (2:17). In all these ways, we see how Paul conceives of the church as participating in temple worship.

Fourth, the church is a people clad in priestly attire. Ephesians 6:10–19 concludes with a military quest and priestly imagery, as it describes the armor of God. First, the "armor of God" (Eph. 6:10) finds its supplier in Isaiah 59:17:

> He put on righteousness as a breastplate,
>   and a helmet of salvation on his head;
> he put on garments of vengeance for clothing,
>   and wrapped himself in zeal as a cloak.

---

4. Gary V. Smith, "Paul's Use of Psalm 68:18 in Ephesians 4:8," *Journal of the Evangelical Theological Society* 18, no. 3 (1975): 187.

5. Cf. Voss, *The Priesthood of All Believers*, 46.

From the background, we are reminded that the servants of God are outfitted as priestly warriors.[6] Like the priestly warfare of Joshua, Christ's gospel mission is a spiritual battle. Therefore, it is vital that the combatants are clothed with holy garments, like priests.

Second, we see in Ephesians 6 the outworking of Psalm 110's military imagery. While Psalm 110:3 pictures the saints clothed in "holy garments" on the "day of your power," verses 5–7 describe the warfare that will come when the royal priest is seated at God's right hand (see Eph. 1:20–21; 2:5). Indeed, when God exalted his Son in heaven and put everything under his feet, he also gave him an army of priests who would worship him and engage in spiritual warfare.[7]

In Colossians 3, Paul also uses clothing imagery to speak of sanctification ("put off" in v. 9; "put on" in vv. 10, 12, 14). And here Paul's language recalls the priestly apparel of Exodus 28. Whereas Aaron's sons were clad in threads of fading glory, those raised in Christ are being renewed in the image of God's glory (Col. 3:10). These image bearers, therefore, must learn to "wear" the glory given to them in Christ (cf. 2 Cor. 3:18).[8] In these verses, the priests of the new covenant are not clothed with literal robes; rather, they are clothed with the holiness that the Spirit of God gives.

Fifth, the church is called to maintain the boundaries of its holy assemblies. In short, church discipline is a priestly activity.[9] To cite one example from Paul where we see this, 1 Corinthians 5 addresses the sin of a man who has taken his father's wife. Paul calls the church to confront this sin and to purge the evil from their midst (vv. 7, 13). In

---

6. Isaiah 59 should be read with Isa. 60–62, which includes Isaiah's promise of future priests (61:5–6).

7. Lest we forget, priests and Levites carried swords as they guarded God's temple. Now, new covenant priests carry the sword of the Spirit, which is the word of God (Eph. 6:17).

8. Cf. Peter J. Leithart, *The Priesthood of the Plebs: A Theology of Baptism* (Eugene, OR: Wipf & Stock, 2003), 107.

9. Anizor and Voss, *Representing Christ*, 135–38.

this chapter, Paul affirms that Christians have authority to exercise discipline not outside the covenant community but within the holy assembly; they are to act like priests who confront sin and remove those who refuse to repent (vv. 11–13). This action is the most severe of the church's priestly actions, and for that reason it requires priests who are trained by God's word and constant in prayer, which leads to another facet of the church's royal priesthood.[10]

The Church Speaks the Words of God

In the Old Testament, priests were given a ministry of word. They taught the law (Lev. 10:11; Deut. 33:9), read the Scriptures (Deut. 31:9–13), and pronounced a blessing over the people (Num. 6:24–26). In the other direction, the priests interceded on behalf of the people and offered prayer as they burned incense (Ps. 141:2). As we saw in the Gospels, Christ took up each of these ministries, and now he shares them with his church. In the letters of Paul and Peter, we find examples of the church focusing on Scripture, praying, and preaching the gospel.

First, the church is called to read and hear Scripture. For instance, in the Pastoral Epistles, Paul regularly commands the church, and especially the overseers, to give attention to "sound doctrine" (e.g., 1 Tim. 1:8–11; 6:2–3; Titus 1:9; 2:1). In 2 Timothy 3:16–17, he declares that all Scripture is God-breathed and profitable for teaching, reproof, correction, and training in righteousness. Moreover, in 1 Timothy 4:13, he tells Timothy, "Devote yourself to the public reading of Scripture, to exhortation, to teaching." This public reading of Scripture is what the priests did in the Old Testament, and now it is the regular practice of the church. The church, as a kingdom

---

10. We should also recognize that baptism is also a priestly activity, as the church welcomes new members into its covenant assembly. Anizor and Voss, *Representing Christ*, 122–28.

of priests, is to hear God's word and instruct one another with it (Rom. 15:14; Eph. 5:15–21; Col. 3:16). Moreover, with the wisdom that comes from Christ (Col. 2:3) and the Holy Spirit (Eph. 5:18), the church is no longer dependent on the Urim and Thummim that hung around the priests' necks. Now, in Christ there is wisdom to make Spirit-led decisions.[11]

Second, the church is called to pray. In almost every letter, Paul begins with a prayer of thanksgiving and concludes with a word of benediction. In between, he often calls the church to pray. In Ephesians 3 he describes the access Christians have to approach their Father in heaven (vv. 12, 14). Later in the same book, he calls the church to pray "at all times in the Spirit, with all prayer and supplication" (6:18). In 1 Thessalonians 5:17–18 he instructs the church to "pray without ceasing" and to "give thanks in all circumstances, for this is the will of the Lord." Likewise, Philippians 4:6 calls the church to make petitions with thanksgiving. Paul also urges men to pray with holy hands in 1 Timothy 2:8, just like priests in passages like Psalm 134:2. Also, in 1 Peter 3:7 and 4:7 respectively, Peter urges husbands to love their wives and Christians to act soberly, for the sake of their prayers. Such attention to holiness and prayer recalls the holy calling of priests entering the temple.

Third, the church is called to proclaim the gospel to others. In addition to reading Scripture and praying, Paul and Peter describe evangelism as a priestly act. For instance, in the verse where the apostle identifies the church as a "royal priesthood" (1 Pet. 2:9), Peter includes a purpose statement: "that you may proclaim the excellencies of him who called you out of darkness into his marvel-

---

11. The use of "lots" in Acts 1:26 may suggest that after the Spirit came, the church no longer needed to rely on the Urim and Thummim for decision-making. Instead, the Spirit granted wisdom to discern God's will, and knowledge to instruct one another.

ous light." Whereas the priests and Levites excluded people from the holy precincts of God, and sheltered themselves from anyone unclean—recall the parable of the good Samaritan, where the priest and the Levite avoided the "dead man" (Luke 10:29–37)—new covenant priests, who are made clean by the Spirit and the blood of Christ, are called to take the gospel to the "unclean" nations. In other words, Christ has made priesthood inclusive, meaning that the gospel cleanses all kinds of people from their sin, drawing them into the temple of God.

Connecting evangelism with its ultimate goal—a royal priesthood composed of all the nations—God's house is founded on Christ by purifying faith (1 Pet. 1:22). The answer to *how* this is possible is that the old covenant has ended, and the new covenant has come, as Isaiah foretold:

> Strangers shall stand and tend your flocks;
>> foreigners shall be your plowmen and vinedressers;
> but you shall be called the priests of the LORD. (61:5–6;
>> cf. 66:21)

Truly, this appears to be Peter's argument. For, after describing the redeeming blood of Christ in 1 Peter 1:18–19, he shares how faith purifies the hearts of God's people (1:22). Thus, with clean hearts, he calls them to love one another (1:22). Next, he urges their holiness (2:1–3), before reminding the elect exiles of their status as a spiritual house, a holy priesthood, a chosen race, a royal priesthood, and a holy nation (2:4–10). From all of these textual clues, Peter indicates that because of Christ, the church is a new covenant priesthood and spiritual temple.

Paul understands his evangelism to the Gentiles in the same way. In Romans 15:16 he describes himself as "a minister of Christ

Jesus to the Gentiles in the priestly service of the gospel of God, so that the offering of the Gentiles may be acceptable, sanctified by the Holy Spirit." What is particularly significant is that when Paul describes his ministry to the Gentiles, he calls it a "priestly service of the gospel of God." With multiple words coming from the temple (e.g., "minister," "priestly service," "offering," "acceptable," "sanctified"), Paul defines his evangelism as priestly. And in an approach to the priesthood that turns the Levitical priesthood upside down (or better, right side up), his gospel ministry includes Gentiles who believe in Christ. While the Old Testament excluded all Gentiles from God's altar (cf. Ezek. 44:6–8), now Paul can speak of the nations as acceptable sacrifices presented to the Lord. Why? Because the Holy Spirit has been given to them, and Jews and Gentiles are one in Christ—a royal priesthood created by the priestly ministry of the gospel (see Eph. 2:11–22).

The Church Offers Spiritual Sacrifices

The last aspect of the priesthood to consider is how the church offers sacrifices to God. To be clear, a Protestant doctrine of the priesthood rejects the Roman Catholic view, where priests are a separate class of clergy whose ministry confers sacramental grace through their service. Indeed, Christ has offered the final sacrifice, and no work of grace can be added to his finished work. That being said, the New Testament speaks of sacrifices that Christians make. These sacrifices are found in their service to one another, their sufferings, and their sharing in the Lord's Supper—not to mention the sacrifice of praise described in Hebrews 13:15–16, which we will consider in the next section. For now, let's see what Paul means by Christian sacrifice.

First, church members serve one another as a priesthood of living sacrifices. In Romans 12, Paul employs priestly language to describe the way Christians respond to the mercies of God.[12] Starting with verses 1–2, Paul writes:

> I appeal to you therefore, brothers, by the mercies of God, to present your bodies as a living sacrifice, holy and acceptable to God, which is your spiritual worship. Do not be conformed to this world, but be transformed by the renewal of your mind, that by testing you may discern what is the will of God, what is good and acceptable and perfect.

It is not a stretch to see God's gifts of grace in verses 3–8 and Paul's instructions of love in verses 9–21 as explaining the priestly sacrifices of verses 1–2. Indeed, Psalms 110 and 132–34 spoke of a day when a brotherhood of priests would gather in joyful worship (110:1–3; 132:9, 16), enjoy spiritual unity (133:1–3), and bless the Lord in the temple together (134:1–3). Now in Christ, Paul is calling the church to brotherly love (Rom. 12:9), jubilant praise (12:10–11), and a ministry of peacemaking (12:16–18). Just as Christ, our great high priest, laid down his life for his church, so we are to do the same. This is what love is (cf. 1 John 3:16). Importantly, one of the abiding metaphors for such loving discipleship is priestly service. We are to offer ourselves as living sacrifices to others, so that they might know God's love through our sacrificial service.

Second, the church offers a living sacrifice as its members suffer for one another. In Colossians 1 Paul describes his gospel ministry, and in verse 24 he states, "Now I rejoice in my sufferings for your sake, and in my flesh I am filling up what is lacking in Christ's afflictions for the sake of his body, that is, the church." This is a difficult verse,

---

12. Voss, *The Priesthood of All Believers*, 144–45, finds six priestly terms in Rom. 12:1 alone: "to offer" ("present"—ESV), "sacrifice," "holy," "acceptable," "spiritual," and "service" ("worship"—ESV). Altogether, the picture is one of priestly service based upon the mercies of the gospel.

but one that is important for understanding the priestly role of God's people. Paul is not saying he is adding something to the atoning work of Christ; he is saying that he is advancing something of the announcement of Christ's work. What is lacking is the message of the gospel and the knowledge of Christ's atoning sacrifice for sin. This is what Paul is suffering for, and he rejoices to suffer for the sake of others' coming to know and believe in Christ.

Such suffering is exemplary in Paul, but it is not restricted to him. As he says in Philippians 1:29, suffering, like faith, is a gift that God grants to all his people. Paul says that he suffers for the sake of the elect (2 Tim. 2:8–11), and throughout the New Testament, suffering is an offering whereby the priests of God prove their faithfulness to God and love to others. Truly, the sword of the priest is no longer sharp and metallic, like it was for the Levites (Ex. 32:25–28) and Phinehas (Num. 25). Rather, the sword of the Spirit is the word of God (Eph. 6:16), and we wage war with the gospel and our lives, not with physical violence. This is a critical distinction between Moses's old covenant priests and Jesus's new covenant priests.

In Israel, the priests were clothed with garments of beauty and glory (Ex. 28:2). But today, the beauty of God's priests is seen in feet that bring good news (Rom. 10:15), and the glory of God's priests is manifest in the way priests are reviled for preaching Christ. As 1 Peter 4:14 states, "If you are insulted for the name of Christ, you are blessed, because the Spirit of glory and of God rests upon you." Such a covering of glory is more lasting than the garments of Aaron, and it rests on the priesthood of believers, who will inherit the kingdom of God.

Third, the church celebrates the sacrifice of Christ when it eats the Lord's Supper. In preparation for the coming kingdom, the priesthood of believers reminds themselves of Christ's sacrificial death and his coming reign. This meal, inaugurated by Jesus on his last night on the earth, is described in 1 Corinthians 10–11. And in these two chapters, we see that this meal joins us to our great high priest (10:14–22), remembers the promises of the new covenant (11:23–26), and requires participants to prepare themselves for the meal and not to eat in an unworthy manner (11:27–32). Such holiness recalls the priestly priority to guard God's house, and it explains why the Lord's Table is the place where church discipline is exercised.

More positively, the Lord's Supper is the place that identifies God's people as a family of priests. In the Old Testament, the priests and the Levites ate the sacrifices offered at the temple. Such access to the offerings was off-limits to the other tribes. To eat from the altar was an incredible privilege. Now, in Christ, the Lord's Supper is a Christian symbol of our priestly access and inheritance. Truly, the Lord's Supper brings to light the priestly identity of the church because it keeps at the center of our gathering the death and resurrection of Jesus Christ, our great high priest.

The Priesthood Explained in Hebrews

From the introduction (1:1–4) to the benediction (13:20–21), Hebrews is dedicated to Christ's high priesthood. And unlike the subtlety of the Gospels or the scattered allusions of Paul, Hebrews shines the spotlight on Christ as God's great high priest. In harmony with the rest of the New Testament, Hebrews does not give a different theology of priesthood. Rather, like the Mount of Transfiguration, Hebrews unveils the glory of Christ hidden by his incarnation. Now that Jesus is resurrected and seated at God's right hand, the unnamed author of Hebrews (henceforth, "the Pastor") blesses the church of Rome with a "word of exhortation" to remain faithful to God's great high priest (13:22–25).

In what follows, I will organize into three categories the Pastor's argument that Jesus is the true and exalted royal priest. First, we will see how the Pastor identifies Christ as the royal priest of Psalm 110. Second, we will observe the qualifications of Christ's priesthood. Third, following our definition of priesthood, we will see how Jesus sanctifies God's Holy Place, speaks God's words, and brings a sacrifice into the heavenly places. Under this final category, we will also consider how Christ shares with his disciples his royal and priestly vocation.

Priestly Identification

As we saw in chapter 4, Psalm 110 is the most important passage in the Old Testament for identifying Christ's priesthood. Now, in Hebrews, we see how this psalm applies to Christ. Importantly, Psalm 110:1 will be cited in Hebrews 1:13, and Psalm 110:4 in Hebrews 5:6. Allusions to Psalm 110 will also be found in Hebrews 1:3; 8:1; 10:12, 13; 12:2 (Ps. 110:1) and Hebrews 5:10; 6:20; 7:3 (Ps. 110:4). In this way, we can see how the royal and priestly themes of this psalm run through Hebrews and identify Christ as a royal priest.

Yet it is not just the use of this psalm that suggests that Jesus is priest. Hebrews regularly calls Jesus a priest. In contrast to the Gospels, where Jesus's priestly status shades the color of the text, in Hebrews Jesus's priesthood is a bright neon sign. To begin with, when Christ's human nature is affirmed in Hebrews 2, verse 17 reads, "Therefore he had to be made like his brothers in every respect, so that he might become a merciful and faithful high priest in the service of God, to make propitiation for the sins of the people." This statement is followed by comparisons between Jesus and Moses (3:1–6) and Jesus and Joshua (4:1–13). Citing the supremacy of Jesus over both of these servants of Yahweh, Hebrews 4:14–16 reiterates the supremacy of Christ's priesthood:

Since then we have a great high priest who has passed through the heavens, Jesus, the Son of God, let us hold fast our confession. For we do not have a high priest who is unable to sympathize with our weaknesses, but one who in every respect has been tempted as we are, yet without sin. Let us then with confidence draw near to the throne of grace, that we may receive mercy and find grace to help in time of need.

These words begin a section of Hebrews that identifies Christ as a priest after the order of Melchizedek (Heb. 5–7). Then the Pastor explains the work of the priest in bringing about a new covenant by way of his superior sacrifice (Heb. 8:1–10:18). And finally, he issues another invitation to come and approach God, saying in Hebrews 10:19–22:

Therefore, brothers, since we have confidence to enter the holy places by the blood of Jesus, by the new and living way that he opened for us through the curtain, that is, through his flesh, and *since we have a great priest over the house of God*, let us draw near with a true heart in full assurance of faith, with our hearts sprinkled clean from an evil conscience and our bodies washed with pure water.

The language of "great high priest" is suggestive of the royal nature of Christ's priesthood. Whereas the kings of Israel had to assign priests to serve at the altar, now Christ is both the king and true priest who lives to intercede for his people. Indeed, it could not be clearer in Hebrews: Jesus is the royal priest to whom all the Scriptures point. He is the substance of whom the Levitical priesthood was a shadow. In fact, making this point all the more clear, we see how the Pastor explains the qualifications of Christ's priesthood.

PRIESTLY QUALIFICATIONS

Throughout this book, we have paid attention to the connection between priests and kings, and a large reason for that comes from Hebrews. If Hebrews did not give us an inspired interpretation of Psalm 110 and Genesis 14, it would be impossible to speak confidently of a royal priest being God's ultimate design. Yet, because Christ's priesthood *is* associated with Melchizedek, the priest-king of Salem, we can confidently understand a biblical theology of priesthood as always having been aimed at something greater than the priesthood of Aaron. Starting in Hebrews 5, the Pastor begins to explain the logic behind a non-Levitical priest.

First, he stresses that priests do not choose themselves for service. Just as God chose Aaron to serve in the tabernacle (vv. 1–4), now God has chosen Christ (vv. 5–10). This heavenly appointment reinforces why Jesus could not call himself a priest during his earthly ministry. As Hebrews 8–9 indicates, Christ's priesthood is located at God's right hand in the heavenly realms (9:11), not in the earthly replica that was given to the Levites (8:5).

Second, Hebrews 5:7–10 recalls the earthly obedience of Jesus—obedience that led to his death on the cross, and obedience that qualified him to serve as priest. Concerning his earthly obedience, the Lord heard his prayer for salvation and granted his request—not by preventing his death but by raising him from the dead. Significantly, the resurrection is the time and place where Jesus is appointed the "Son" of God (Heb. 5:5; cf. Acts 13:32–33; Rom. 1:4). According to Hebrews 5:5–10, Jesus's resurrection, combined with his ascension to God's right hand, is the time when Jesus is "designated by God a high priest after the order of Melchizedek" (v. 10). Indeed, it is through Jesus perfect "reverence" that his prayers are heard (v. 7), and it is in his "being made perfect" that Christ takes on the role of high priest (vv. 9–10).

Important for the argument of Hebrews is the language of perfection found in verse 9 and elsewhere.[13] In Hebrews, Christ's perfection describes his "indestructible life" that comes in his resurrection (see 7:16). When Christ was raised from the dead, he was "made perfect forever" (7:28), and hence is able to hold his "priesthood permanently" and "save to the uttermost those who draw near to God through him, since he always lives to make intercession for them" (7:24–25). This is what sets Jesus apart from the Levitical priests, which is what Hebrews 7 outlines in great detail.

Third, Jesus's qualification for priesthood is explained in relationship to the Levitical priesthood. In Hebrews 7:1–10, the Pastor gives an exposition of Genesis 14, where he identifies the superiority of Melchizedek over Levi by way of Abraham's dealings with the priest-king of Salem. On this reading, the Levitical priesthood (which describes the sons of Aaron) is inferior to Melchizedek's. Next, Hebrews 7:11–28 traces the intrinsic weakness of Aaron and his sons to the fact that they die (v. 23), and even as they live, they sin and must offer sacrifices for themselves (v. 27). By contrast, Jesus's priesthood is based upon his perfection, his indestructible life, and God's sworn oath to him. Jesus is the priest after the order of Melchizedek, and hence he is greater than any and all of the Levitical priests. As verses 26–28 conclude:

> It was indeed fitting that we should have such a high priest, holy, innocent, unstained, separated from sinners, and exalted above the heavens. He has no need, like those high priests, to offer sacrifices daily, first for his own sins and then for those of the people, since he did this once for all when he offered up himself. For the law appoints men in their weakness as high priests, but the word of the oath,

---

13. See Heb. 2:10; 7:11, 19, 28; 9:9, 11; 10:1, 14; 11:40; 12:2, 23.

which came later than the law, appoints a Son who has been
made perfect forever.

Priestly Actions

After seeing the connections between Jesus and Psalm 110, as well as
the qualifications for his priesthood, we turn to see Jesus's priesthood
in action. As a priest forever after the order of Melchizedek, Jesus
performs a ministry superior to all others. And in his sanctifying of
God's house, speaking God's word, and sacrificing for sin, we will
see why.

First, Jesus sanctifies God's Holy Place. In Leviticus, there is one
offering that sanctified God's house. It is the Day of Atonement, the
ceremony where the high priest came with blood to purify the mercy
seat in the Most Holy Place (Lev. 16). As we saw in chapter 2, this annual event was central to Leviticus and to the whole priestly calendar.
In Hebrews, the Day of Atonement is central to understanding what
Christ's death has accomplished for the dwelling place of God too.
Only, Jesus's sanctification of God's temple purifies the real thing—
not just a type.

In Hebrews 9:6–14 we discover that Jesus's sacrifice functions
as a greater Day of Atonement, as he enters the tent not made with
hands (v. 11)—that is, the true and heavenly tabernacle, where God
himself dwells. Indeed, the Levitical priests purified a shadow of
God's throne room when they entered the Most Holy Place (vv. 6–7),
but Jesus entered heaven itself. As Hebrews 9:24 puts it, "Christ has
entered, not into holy places made with hands, which are copies of
the true things, but into heaven itself, now to appear in the presence
of God on our behalf."

Whereas the Levitical priests purified the copies of heavenly
things (Heb. 8:5; 9:23), Jesus has purified the real. Therefore, he did

not have to cleanse it again. Moreover, because he has entered heaven to stay—unlike the priests who entered the Most Holy Place to leave—when Jesus brought his offering into heaven, it was finished, once and for all (Heb. 9:26). In this way, we see that Jesus's priestly action toward God's dwelling place far exceeds the purification rites of the old covenant—a theme that pervades Hebrews 8–9.

At the same time, Jesus not only cleanses heaven; he is also bringing holiness to earth. This is seen in the way he opposes Satan, that great unclean serpent that Adam failed to throw out of God's garden. Speaking of Christ's sacrifice in terms of warfare and victory, Hebrews 2:14–15 reads, "He himself likewise partook of the same things, that through death he might destroy the one who has the power of death, that is, the devil, and deliver all those who through fear of death were subject to lifelong slavery."

Like the most faithful priests in Israel's history (e.g., Phinehas, Jehoiada, Azariah), Jesus not only has offered a sacrifice for sin on the cross; he has also taken up arms to defeat Satan. In ascending to God's right hand, Jesus has driven Satan out of God's presence, thus purifying God's throne.[14] And now Jesus is commanding from God's right hand (Ps. 110:1–4) a kingdom of priests on earth to bring the gospel to Jew and Gentile alike. This warfare is spiritual, not militaristic. Jesus is sending his word and his Spirit throughout the lands to deliver his people from the enemy. This is the warfare described in Psalm 110.

This warfare is mentioned in Hebrews 10:12–13, where the Pastor alludes to Psalm 110 and says, "But when Christ had offered for all time a single sacrifice for sins, he sat down at the right hand of God, *waiting from that time until his enemies should be*

---

14. It should be remembered that in the Old Testament, unclean spirits had access to the throne of God in heaven (1 Kings 22:19–23; Job 1:6–12). This changed when Christ ascended to God's right hand and threw Satan down (cf. Rev. 12:12–17; 20:1–6).

made a footstool for his feet." Today, Christ has finished his work in heaven, but his work on earth continues, as he prays for his people and teaches them his written word. These are priestly actions that we have seen throughout the Bible, and now we see them in Hebrews too.

Second, Christ prays for and speaks to his people. First, Hebrews 7:25 says, Christ "always lives to make intercession for them." In context, this "always lives" relates to Christ's indestructible resurrection life. In practice, this means that our high priest does not need to spend time on himself, offering sacrifices for his sins or worrying about his impending death. Rather, Jesus's ongoing ministry in heaven is one of intercession for his people on earth, until every enemy is put down (Heb. 10:13) and every child of God is brought home (Heb. 9:28).

Jesus's priestly intercession is matched by his ministry of teaching. In Hebrews 1:1–2 we are told that his word is greater than all the Prophets. He is the full and final revelation of God, and as the rest of Hebrews 1:1–2:4 explains, "we must pay much closer attention to what we have heard" (2:1). Indeed, while he was on earth, Jesus taught his disciples. Acts 1:1 insinuates that he continues to teach us. And in Hebrews, the testimony is repeated. God's word is living and active (4:12); the Spirit continues to speak (3:7); and through the apostles and prophets whom he inspired, Jesus continues to perform a ministry of teaching. In fact, Christ's words do not merely give us information; Hebrews 4:13–16 indicates how they uncover us and command us to draw near. As Hebrews 3:1 says, Jesus is "the apostle and high priest of our confession." In other words, Jesus is the one sent by God to build up his house with his word (3:1–6), and we do well to listen to his teaching—teaching that always brings us back to his priestly sacrifice for sins.

SACRIFICING FOR GOD'S PEOPLE

The last priestly action of Christ is the one that is most important—namely, Jesus's sacrificial offering, which (1) makes a way for us to approach God, (2) redeems God's people from the curse of the law, (3) inaugurates a new covenant, (4) cleanses the conscience, and (5) makes God's people a kingdom of priests in their own right. In these five aspects of Christ's sacrifice, we learn much about what Christ has accomplished in his priestly offering.

First, Hebrews 4:14–16 and 10:19–22 indicate that Christ's priestly offering makes a way for God's people to approach God. By vocation, priests are invited to draw near. But under the Old Testament, they did that on behalf of others. Now, however, because of Christ's greater sacrifice and his permanent place at God's right hand, he invites his people to draw near to the throne of grace (4:16) by means of the veil he tore in his own torn flesh (10:20).

Second, Christ's sacrifice puts an end to all the curses accrued under the old covenant. As Hebrews 9:15 states, "A death has occurred that redeems them from the transgressions committed under the first covenant." Because Christ perfectly obeyed God (Heb. 10:1–10), his death was not a punishment for his own sins. Rather, it was the self-offering of himself for others. Because of his obedience unto death, he became the "source of eternal salvation," having "learned obedience through what he suffered" (Heb. 5:8–9), which is a reference to his death on the cross.

Third, in the same moment that Christ's death put to death the curses of the law (Heb. 9:15–17), he also inaugurated a new covenant (9:15–22). Referring back to the covenant at Sinai (9:20), the Pastor explains how Christ's blood initiates a new covenant. The stipulations of Jeremiah's new covenant are cited in Hebrews 8:8–13 (Jer. 31:31–34), and in Hebrews 8–9 he explains how Christ's superior sacrifice enacts a better covenant with better promises—namely, a covenant that secures forgiveness for all those whom Christ serves as their mediator. Earlier in Hebrews, the Pastor recalled the weakness of Moses and Joshua, and how their service failed to bring people into the place of God's rest. The people died in their unbelief, and their sins prevented them from drawing near to God. By contrast, Jesus has initiated a covenant that guarantees forgiveness and makes access to God possible.

Fourth, the superiority of Christ's sacrifice is also seen in the way he cleanses the conscience. As Hebrews 9:13–14 states,

> If the blood of goats and bulls, and the sprinkling of defiled persons with the ashes of a heifer, sanctify for the purification of the flesh, how much more will the blood of Christ, who through the eternal Spirit offered himself without blemish to God, purify our conscience from dead works to serve the living God.

In its time, the Levitical system achieved what it was designed to do—Yahweh dwelt among the people of Israel, and Israel enjoyed his presence. Ultimately, this system proved insufficient; it did not cleanse the conscience, and time and again it foundered. In Christ, however, we find a sacrifice that cleanses the conscience and prepares the people of God to serve as royal priests in their own right.

Fifth, the last thing to mention about Christ's sacrifice is the ongoing effect it has on the church. As mentioned above, the Levitical priests drew near to God's presence with fear and trembling. Never would a faithful priest under the old covenant have considered bringing another into the Most Holy Place. Yet now, through Christ's sacrifice, a new and living way has been made, such that all those in Christ may draw near to God themselves (Heb. 4:14–16; 10:19–22).

This access to God's throne confers on all of God's people the blessed status of royal priests. In fact, what is said of Jesus in the beginning of Hebrews is also said of the people by the end.

In Hebrews 1:1–3, Jesus is called the Son of God; he is described as the royal heir of the world; and he is granted a position to sit at God's right hand after making purification for sins. Indeed, in the opening words of Hebrews, Jesus is a son, a king, and a priest. By the end of Hebrews, the same vocations are assigned to those who trust in Christ. In Hebrews 12:1–18, we see that God's sons must be willing to receive their father's discipline (cf. Heb. 2:10–18). In Hebrews 12:19–29, we find discussion about the kingdom that God is bringing into the world, and here the believing saints are promised a place on Mount Zion (vv. 22–24). Last, in Hebrews 13:1–19, the book concludes with a description of the believer's life as fundamentally priestly. Verses 10–16, in particular, call us to eat the food of the altar and offer a sacrifice of praise. These are both priestly actions, and importantly, they are not just something Jesus has done. They are the priestly calling of every follower of Christ too.

In short, Hebrews closes with instructions for Christians to live their lives as a family of royal priests. This is ultimately what Christ's sacrifice has accomplished—it has redeemed a people who are to live as royal priests in this age and in the age to come. Jesus is the great high priest to whom all the Scriptures point, and now he is assembling a priesthood who will be with him forever in his kingdom. This is where Hebrews ends, and it leads us to the book of Revelation, our final stop in this biblical theology of the royal priesthood.

The Priesthood Everlasting in Revelation

By the time we arrive at Revelation, we have seen how the rest of the New Testament has asserted Christ's victory over the powers and principalities (see, e.g., Col. 2:13–15; Heb. 2:14–18), celebrated

Christ's ascension as God's high priest (Acts 1:9–11; 2:33–34; Eph. 1:21–22; Col. 3:1–4; Heb. 5:1–10; 7:1–28; 12:2), and commissioned Christ's kingdom of priests as evangelistic warriors (cf. Eph. 6:10–19). Therefore, in reading Revelation as the capstone of the biblical canon, we have good reason for seeing royal priesthood in Revelation in a similar light.

In the three places where Revelation mentions priesthood directly (1:6; 5:9–10; 20:6), we find a unified vision of the church between Christ's resurrection and return. While the church seems defeated, Revelation explains the true reality of the church militant. Those who abide in faith are the true conquerors, a kingdom of priests in service to God. Even more, in this apocalyptic letter the sevenfold structure of Revelation keeps returning us to the heavenly temple of God, where we hear the voice of Jesus, the high priest, speaking from the throne (1:4–8). Indeed, the whole book provides a heavenly vision of God's royal priesthood on earth.[15] In what follows, we will consider three aspects of the priesthood in this final book.

First, the kingdom of priests is created by the sacrifice of Christ. In Revelation 1:6 John introduces the risen Christ, saying, "To him who loves us and has freed us from our sins by his blood and made us a kingdom, priests to his God and Father, to him be glory and dominion forever and ever." Likewise, Revelation 5:9–10 sings praise to the Lamb:

> Worthy are you to take the scroll
> >and to open its seals,
> for you were slain, and by your blood you ransomed people
> >>for God
> >>from every tribe and language and people and nation,

---

15. On the approach to Revelation taken here, see Richard Bauckham, *The Theology of the Book of Revelation* (New York: Cambridge University Press, 1993), 1–22.

> and you have made them a kingdom and priests to our God,
>
> and they shall reign on the earth.

Together, these verses indicate that royal priesthood is not achieved by man but received from Christ's work on the cross. Conveying the twin themes of sacrifice and victory, these verses teach how Christ's priestly sacrifice atones for the sins of his people *and* grants them authority to reign with him as priests in his kingdom. Indeed, victory is a key theme in Revelation, one meant to strengthen faith and stir up Christ-centered worship.[16] But, importantly, victory is not an end in itself but a source of priestly worship and service in God's temple. Hence, priestly service is what Christians do on earth and in heaven.

Second, Christ is a royal priest who radiates the glory of God. As with the Gospels, Jesus is not named a priest in Revelation, yet his priestly glory shines throughout. For instance, Jesus is presented in robes of glory—just like the priests of Israel (1:12–16; cf. Ex. 28:2; Matt. 17:2).[17] Next, as "one like a son of man," he stands "in the midst of the lampstands" (Rev. 1:13). This describes Jesus's presence in the churches using priestly imagery (Rev. 1:20)—meaning, just as priests walked before the lampstands in the tabernacle (Num. 8:1–4), so Jesus is presented walking before his lampstands here. Third, the repeated use of "Lamb" indicates the effective sacrifice he offered to defeat his enemies and save his people.[18] This coheres with the exodus themes that run through the book of Revelation, which is what made Israel a kingdom of priests in the first place. Far superior to Moses, whose song appears in Revelation 15:3, Jesus has led his

---

16. See the repeated word of "victory" to those who conquer by faith (Rev. 2:7, 11, 17, 26; 3:5, 12, 21). Interestingly, each of these promises bears a priestly reward.

17. The priestly glory of Christ continues to punctuate the descriptions of Christ among the churches (see Rev. 2:1, 8, 12, 18; 3:1, 7, 14).

18. "Lamb" is used twenty-eight times to describe Christ in Revelation (see 5:6, 8, 12, 13; 6:1, 16; 7:9, 10, 14, 17; 12:11; 13:8; 14:1, 4 [2x], 10; 15:3; 17:14 [2x]; 19:7, 9; 21:9, 14, 22, 23, 27; 22:1, 3).

brothers into the presence of God and made them a kingdom of priests. All in all, God's glory radiates throughout Revelation, as it celebrates the kingdom of God, which has come to earth by means of Christ's priestly sacrifice.

Third, God's royal priests engage in worship and warfare. In Revelation 5:9–10, the focus is worship—those in heaven praise God for Christ's work on earth. The redeemed on earth also worship God (not the beast), but for them worship means warfare. In other words, as Revelation describes the spiritual battle on earth, it becomes clear that those who suffer for the sake of the Lamb are true priests in God's kingdom. Accordingly, when Revelation 20:6 says, "Blessed and holy is the one who shares in the first resurrection! Over such the second death has no power, but they will be priests of God and of Christ, and they will reign with him for a thousand years," we should see this as a call to arms (cf. Rev. 19:11–16).[19] In truth, Christ's reign is nothing but protested on the earth, but for those redeemed by the Lamb, their priestly calling is to bear witness to God's king.

From Paul and Peter, we have seen how evangelism is a priestly occupation. Here in Revelation, John uses military language to speak of the battle that comes against Christ's people. Yet, like Christ, we do not wage war with worldly weapons. As priests we worship, pray, serve, and witness. Just as Psalm 110 indicated, when the high priest takes his place at God's right hand, his people purchased by his blood will go to war—proclaiming the gospel of the kingdom and waging war with prayer and patience. As Derek Kidner says of Psalm 110:5–7, "We have moved on from Hebrews to Revelation, where the

---

19. In Rev. 1:12–16 Jesus wore priestly garments of glory and beauty in the midst of the church. Now he wears priestly garments onto the battlefield, just like the divine warrior envisioned in Isa. 59. In this case, he is joined by his saints, who are also clothed in white robes (Rev. 19:7–8) and called upon to serve with him as a heavenly army (Rev. 19:14). Revelation portrays Jesus as the Ps. 110 high priest, leading his purified people into battle.

picture of judgment and victory is no less terrible than that of verse 6 (cf. e.g., Rev 19:11–21)."[20]

Revelation expands this priestly vision and ends with the promise of a new creation. As G. K. Beale has put it, the Bible ends where it begins: "It begins with a pristine creation over which a priest-king rules for God's glory and ends with a new-creational kingdom where a priest-king rules with his followers (who are subordinate kings and priests) for God's glory."[21] Indeed, by means of tracing royal priesthood through the Bible, we are able to better understand the heavenly vision of Revelation. At the same time, however, this graphic account of redemptive history gives us a climactic vision of glory that centers on Jesus Christ—the long-awaited Son of God, who is the King of kings, Lord of lords, and Priest of priests.

Truly, Jesus is worthy of all praise, glory, honor, and power. And amazingly, as the true high priest, he shares that glory with all those who follow him on his priestly path of obedience. By guarding God's holiness, testifying to God's word, and trusting in God's Son, the priests in Christ's kingdom display God's glory on earth as it is in heaven. In this way, the fullness of Christ's royal priesthood will be formed in us, and his glory will be seen on the earth as it now fills heaven.

20. Derek Kidner, *Psalms 73–150*, Tyndale Old Testament Commentaries (Downers Grove, IL: IVP Academic, 2008), 430–31.

21. G. K. Beale, *A New Testament Biblical Theology: The Unfolding of the Old Testament in the New* (Grand Rapids, MI: Baker Academic, 2011), 167–68.

Epilogue

Royal Priesthood Yesterday,
Today, and Forever

As I came to the end of writing this book, I sat in a room full of royal priests and wept. I had not slipped into some clandestine temple or agreed to join a society with secret handshakes and funny hats. I had simply gone to a men's breakfast at church, where a priest of God was teaching about leadership from the book of Deuteronomy. As he made his closing remarks, he drew our attention to Deuteronomy 17:18–20, and the vision of this Israelite king stirred my soul with new affection:

> And when he sits on the throne of his kingdom, he shall write for himself in a book a copy of this law, approved by the Levitical priests. And it shall be with him, and he shall read in it all the days of his life, that he may learn to fear the LORD his God by keeping all the words of this law and these statutes, and doing them, that his heart may not be lifted up above his brothers, and that he may not turn aside from the commandment, either to the right hand or to the

left, so that he may continue long in his kingdom, he and
his children, in Israel.

While listening, I could not help but tie together this passage with
everything this book has tried to envision. Reading Deuteronomy 17
with Christ's royal priesthood in mind resulted in a flash of glory.
Consider: When Moses describes the king of Israel, this servant of
God was to write down the law under the supervision of Levitical
priests and to teach it to his sons. This practice was meant to ensure
that his rule would be righteous, even priestly. The effect would be a
priestly king ruling his people with compassion as he established his
throne in righteousness.

In Israel's history, the reality of Deuteronomy 17 happened rarely,
if ever. As 2 Chronicles 35:18 recalls: "No Passover like it had been
kept in Israel since the days of Samuel the prophet. None of the kings
of Israel had kept such a Passover as was kept by Josiah, and the
priests and the Levites, and all Judah and Israel who were present,
and the inhabitants of Jerusalem." If any king had written the law
of God as Moses prescribed, he would have transcribed Deuteronomy 16 and its instructions for Passover. That the Passover had not
been kept since the time of Samuel indicates the inconsistency of
God's people and the weakness of the law to reform priests and kings.

As this book has presented, no heir of David or son of Aaron ever
matched Adam's glory. But in the coming of Christ, the Last Adam
sat down at the right hand of the Father. As a result, Jesus fulfilled
Psalm 110 and the promise of a king who would keep the law. Indeed,
because Christ perfectly fulfilled the Law and the Prophets, he has
proved his right to be God's high priest. And more than transcrib-
ing God's law for himself (Deut. 17:18), he embodies it *and* writes it
on the hearts of his brothers and sisters (Jer. 31:33). Seated in glory,
Christ sends his Spirit and his word to complete his priestly work.

Perfect in sacrifice and in speech, Jesus teaches everyone whom he represents as high priest (Isa. 54:13; Ezek. 36:26–27). This is the promise of the new covenant he mediates as the royal priest and the source of God's glorious gospel.

As we have seen in this biblical theology of the royal priesthood, what the Old Testament patterned, legislated, promised, and anticipated has now arrived in Christ. Hebrews explains how Jesus is a royal priest, and the rest of the New Testament identifies the church as his family of royal priests. Today, Jesus is in his heavenly temple, and simultaneously he is building his house on earth. Wonderfully, kingdom and priesthood have come together in Christ and will never be separated. Truly, Christ's royal priesthood reveals the glory of God on earth as it is in heaven.

Returning to the opening scenes of this book, God's story of royal priesthood is larger than any theater can capture. Indeed, only the entire cosmos in all of human history is able to reflect the glory of the royal priesthood that God is establishing in Christ. This priestly narrative covers the entire Bible, and its drama repeats every time churches gather on earth to worship God in heaven.

From the rising of the sun to its setting, wherever the gospel of the kingdom has redeemed sinners and raised them to life in Christ, the children of God are learning to live out their priestly calling. And whether or not they think of themselves as priests, their actions identify who they are. In worshiping God, serving one another, sanctifying God's house with prayer and church discipline, baptizing saints, communing at the Lord's Table, offering sacrifices of praise, speaking the word to one another, and blessing the nations with the gospel, they are priests living in the kingdom of Christ.

This way of life is the one that brings glory to God and extends Jesus's blessing to the ends of the earth. Because of Christ's priesthood, heaven and earth have been united in Christ. And one day soon, as Psalm 110 foretells, all Christ's enemies will be put under his feet. But until then, let us fix our eyes on God's Son, our great high priest, so that we, who are priests in his kingdom, might receive his blessing—a blessing that Jesus takes up and speaks over all his people, the ones for whom he lives to intercede:

> The Lord bless you and keep you;
> the Lord make his face to shine upon you and be gracious
>   to you;
> the Lord lift up his countenance upon you and give you
>   peace. (Num. 6:24–26)

General Index

Scripture Index

Short Studies in Biblical Theology Series

THE SON OF GOD
AND THE NEW CREATION
GRAEME GOLDSWORTHY

MARRIAGE
AND THE MYSTERY OF THE GOSPEL
RAY ORTLUND

WORK
AND OUR LABOR IN THE LORD
JAMES M. HAMILTON JR.

COVENANT
AND GOD'S PURPOSE FOR THE WORLD
THOMAS R. SCHREINER

THE CITY OF GOD
AND THE GOAL OF CREATION
T. DESMOND ALEXANDER

THE KINGDOM OF GOD
AND THE GLORY OF THE CROSS
PATRICK SCHREINER

FROM CHAOS TO COSMOS
CREATION TO NEW CREATION
SIDNEY GREIDANUS

THE LORD'S SUPPER
AS THE SIGN AND MEAL OF THE NEW COVENANT
GUY PRENTISS WATERS

REDEMPTIVE REVERSALS
AND THE IRONIC OVERTURNING OF HUMAN WISDOM
G. K. BEALE

DIVINE BLESSING
AND THE FULLNESS OF LIFE IN THE PRESENCE OF GOD
WILLIAM R. OSBORNE

THE SERPENT
AND THE SERPENT SLAYER
ANDREW DAVID NASELLI

THE NEW CREATION
AND THE STORYLINE OF SCRIPTURE
FRANK THIELMAN

THE ROYAL PRIESTHOOD
AND THE GLORY OF GOD
DAVID S. SCHROCK

For more information, visit **crossway.org/ssbt**.